Lifeline

BIOGRAPHIES

DANICA PATRICK
Racing's Trailblazer

by Karen Sirvaitis

Twenty-First Century Books · Minneapolis

Twenty-First Century Books
A division of Lerner Publishing Group, Inc.
241 First Avenue North
Minneapolis, MN 55401 U.S.A.

Website address: www.lernerbooks.com

Library of Congress Cataloging-in-Publication Data

Sirvaitis, Karen 1961–
    Danica Patrick / by Karen Sirvaitis.
        p.   cm. — (USA TODAY lifeline biographies)
    Includes bibliographical references and index.
    ISBN 978-0-7613-5222-8 (lib. bdg. : alk. paper)
    1. Patrick, Danica, 1982– —Juvenile literature. 2. Automobile racing drivers—United
States—Biography—Juvenile literature. 3. Women automobile racing drivers—United
States—Biography—Juvenile literature. I. Title.
GV1032.P38C37 2011
796.72092—dc22 [B]   2009045846

Manufactured in the United States of America
1 – VI – 7/15/10

INTRODUCTION

Track face: Danica Patrick heads to her car for the start of the Indianapolis 500 on May 29, 2005.

Danica Mania

"Lady and gentlemen, start your engines!"

The announcer signaled drivers to rev up their motors at the Indianapolis Motor Speedway in Indianapolis, Indiana. The date was May 29, 2005. The race was the Indy 500, one of the most popular competitions in North America. The lady was twenty-three-year-old Danica Patrick.

Like the other racing teams planning to enter the Indy 500, Danica and her team showed up in Indianapolis early in the month of May. They spent the month doing practice runs, fine-tuning their strategy, stocking the pit stop with tools and equipment. They needed to be one of the top thirty-three teams to qualify for the race. During qualifying rounds, racers do their best to record fast times so they can earn a good starting position.

 Indy 500 is short for the Indianapolis 500-Mile Race. It is one of the oldest motorsport events in North America. For years, it has been billed as The Greatest Spectacle in Racing®.

Danica was fairly new to the world of professional racing. But over the course of the month, she proved she could be stiff competition. During a practice session on May 12, 2005, Danica logged the fastest time of all the drivers, reaching a top speed of 229.880 miles per hour (369.956 kilometers per hour). She was the fourth-fastest qualifying driver, earning a starting position of fourth place. More and more people started to pay attention to Danica. Who was this young newcomer?

First-time driver: Danica logs her first laps on the Indianapolis Motor Speedway in preparation for the 2005 Indy 500.

Indy first: In 2005 Danica became the first woman to lead a lap in the Indy 500.

On race day, Danica continued to impress fans. During lap fifty-seven of two hundred, she slid into first place, becoming the first woman ever to lead a lap in the Indy 500. With ten laps to go, Danica took the lead again and the crowd went crazy. The cheering became louder than the noise of the cars zooming around the oval. Were they about to witness history? Was Danica going to be the first woman to win the Indy 500?

IN FOCUS

No Women Allowed

For the first forty years of the Indianapolis Motor Speedway, women were welcome only as spectators. The racetrack, pit areas, and even the press box were off limits. In 1956 the speedway let a female reporter into the press box for the first time. Fifteen years later, a different female reporter sued the speedway for being banned from areas of the track that male reporters could access. She won the case. Since 1971 the speedway has allowed women to enter all areas of the speedway, including the track.

www.usatoday.com

USA TODAY

Sports
SECTION C

May 31, 2005

Wheels of progress
turn slowly for women

**From the Pages of
USA TODAY**

As a foremother who had watched a young woman leave a parade of men in her Indy 500 dust, Billie Jean King was moved to dial up Janet Guthrie for a pioneer-to-pioneer chat. Without you, King would tell Guthrie's answering machine, there could not have been a Danica.

No, there could not have been a Danica Patrick had Guthrie, Lyn St. James and Sarah Fisher not come before her, just as there could not have been an Annika Sörenstam at the Colonial had King not swatted Bobby Riggs over the Astrodome wall. A quarter century after that epic 1973 gender bender, King watched the tape for the first time and was struck by the commentary heard by 50 million viewers. "Howard Cosell only talked about my looks," she recalled Monday. "That's what kills us as athletes. Just once, talk only about our accomplishments. That's all we ask."

Apparently King and her court are asking for too much. Patrick had to be covered differently, as she delivered the best female finish ever at the 500. That's history. That's news. But the fact she might be described as a "babe" has nothing to do with her performance behind the wheel of a machine traveling 226 miles an hour [364 km/h]. "We want a chance to be the best we can be," King said. "We just want to be let in. Just let us in."

—Ian O'Connor

Battle of the sexes: Tennis player Bobby Riggs challenged Billie Jean King to a match in 1973. He boasted that, as a male, he was certain to win. King *(above)* trounced him.

With six laps remaining, Danica was low on fuel. Stopping to refuel would take her out of the lead for certain. To finish the race, Danica would have to conserve what little amount she had left. She slowed down just a bit. One car passed her and then another and another. Within a matter of seconds, Danica went from first to fourth place—the same position in which she had started the race.

In the Indy 500, racers drive in excess of 200 miles per hour (322 kilometers per hour) 200 times around a 2.5-mile (4 km) oval track.

Danica didn't win. She didn't even come in second. But as a fourth place female rookie, Danica got the world's attention. Danica had just set a couple of racing records. Fourth place was the best finish ever for a woman in the Indy 500. And she became the first woman to lead not only one but nineteen laps, as she fell in and out of first place.

Danica wasn't the first woman to race in the Indy 500. But she was the only woman in the race that day.

Congratulations: Danica and team owner Bobby Rahal celebrate her record-breaking finish in 2005.

In the speedway's ninety-four-year history, only three other women had raced the track. Fast and dangerous, race car driving has always been a male-dominated sport. For many years, women weren't even allowed to race the Indy 500.

IN FOCUS

Breaking Barriers

Janet Guthrie (born 1938) was an aerospace engineer from Iowa City, Iowa. Guthrie worked for the National Aeronautics and Space Administration (NASA) and almost became an astronaut. Although she never got the opportunity to break out of Earth's orbit, she did break gender barriers on the racetrack. In 1977 Guthrie became the first woman to race in the Indy 500.

One of Guthrie's hobbies was racing Jaguars. Race car team owner Rolla Vollstedt recognized her talent. In 1977 Vollstedt entered Guthrie in the Indy 500. She had to exit the race because of mechanical difficulties. But she returned to the Indy 500 in 1978 to finish in ninth place.

In the twenty-eight-year period between Guthrie's and Danica's races, only two other women qualified for the Indy 500. They are Lyn St. James and Sarah Fisher. In 2007 Milka Duno became the fifth female Indy 500 driver.

First female qualifier: Janet Guthrie celebrates qualifying for the Indy 500 in 1977.

Something to smile about: Danica talks to a reporter about her historic fourth-place finish at the 2005 Indy 500.

The attention Danica got was mind-boggling. Retailers sold more Danica merchandise than they had for any single racer throughout the speedway's history. Fans bought an unbelievable amount of Danica Patrick t-shirts, hats, and other items. They were hungry for all things Danica. Hundreds of newspaper, radio, and TV interviews kept Danica in the public eye.

Danica Mania had begun.

Illinois fields: Danica grew up in Roscoe, Illinois. Roscoe is a suburb (of Rockford, Illinois) of about nine thousand people directly south of Illinois' border with Wisconsin. The town is surrounded by corn and soybean fields.

The Starting Line

■■■■

Danica Sue Patrick was born on March 25, 1982, in Beloit, a small town in southern Wisconsin. She grew up just south of Beloit, in the town of Roscoe, Illinois. Roscoe is a fast-growing suburb, but when Danica was born, only a few thousand people lived there.

From Danica's childhood, no one would have guessed she'd become a national celebrity. She hung out with her younger sister Brooke, made cookies with her mom, and played with Barbie dolls. She also spent a

A racing family: Danica, her mother Bev *(left)*, and her father T. J. *(right)* pose after a race in 2008.

great deal of time watching her dad, T. J., enjoy one of his hobbies—working on race cars. "Thanks to him," Danica later wrote, "I grew up thinking about things most other ten-year-old girls aren't even aware of, such as RPMs [revolutions per minute, a measure of how rapidly an engine works]."

T. J. wasn't the only mechanic in the family. He and Danica's mother, Bev, first met at a snowmobile race. T. J. was a racer, and Bev was a mechanic for a female racer. The couple was attracted to all things fast and adventurous. But when they settled down to have children, they also had two businesses—a plate glass manufacturing company and a coffee shop. Their responsibilities at work and as parents didn't leave much time for adventure.

In 1992 when Danica was ten and Brooke was eight, Bev and T. J. started thinking that they needed to spend more time together as a family. They had set aside some money and decided to buy a pontoon boat. The boat wouldn't give them the adventure they missed, but it would give them a chance to spend some time on the water with their girls.

But the girls had other ideas. After trying out a friend's go-kart, they told their parents they wanted to try go-kart racing, or karting. Bev and T. J. didn't take much convincing. Racing sounded like something the entire family might enjoy. The girls' parents set aside their plans to purchase the pontoon boat and bought two racing karts instead. Brooke was excited about the idea and couldn't wait to get started. Danica, less enthused, went along for the ride.

 A race car builder named Art Ingels built the first go-kart in 1956. He put together pieces of scrap metal and then added a small engine. Before long, other people started building karts and meeting to race.

Crash!

To give the girls some practice, T. J. set up a trail of paint cans to form a race course in the parking lot of the family business. Shortly after buckling up in her new kart for the first time, Danica found herself facing a wall. Going 25 miles per hour (40 km/h), she hit it head-on when her kart's brakes failed to work. Terrified, Danica's father sprinted over to his daughter. But Danica was fine. She had wrecked the kart, but all she could talk about was when she could get a new one.

Despite crashing the first time she rode her kart, Danica fell in love with the sport. "The exhilaration I felt when I stepped on the pedal of my first go-kart was enough to hook me for life. I loved steering my kart around tight corners and barreling down the straightaways.

Bumper-to-bumper: Even at a young age level, go-kart racing can be very competitive.

Woo hoo! At age ten, I had found my life's passion. From that point forward I had a one-track mind . . . I dedicated myself to becoming the best race-car driver in the world."

Unstoppable

In 1992 Danica and Brooke joined the World Karting Association (WKA), a group that organizes races for kids ages eight through sixteen. The WKA places a racer according to age, weight, and the size of his or her engine. Both girls were in the Junior Sportsman Stock class for ages eight through twelve. Danica and her sister were the only girl racers in the group. T. J. had one rule for the girls: if they wanted to race, they had to learn something about the kart or about racing each time they went out on the track.

Part of the fun in karting was gearing up. Danica had a black kart. To stand out on the track, she wore a purple and lime green suit with D-A-N-I-C-A spelled out across the front. Gearing up could also be uncomfortable. In addition to a driving suit, kart drivers have to wear gloves, full face helmets, and boots that go over the ankles. Danica had to stuff her long hair into her helmet, making her head sweat and itch during a race. But she didn't care. She was having fun.

After only six months of racing, Danica was setting records at Sugar River Raceway, her local karting track. It didn't take long for Danica to taste her first victory on the Sugar River track, either. On one early weekend, Danica was in third place with two laps to go. All of a sudden, the two karts ahead of her crashed into each other. Although the drivers were safe, their vehicles needed major repairs. They were out of the race. Danica swerved around the crash site and maintained the lead for the remaining laps. The excitement she felt when crossing the finish line was overwhelming. Danica had won, and she loved the feeling.

A Hunch

After several races, Brooke lost interest in karting. She did, however, enjoy watching her sister compete. Every week Danica seemed to improve. She followed her father's advice about racing strategy. She took the sport seriously. She tried to work harder than her competition. She kept a winning attitude. And she made a point to learn something every time she raced, whether it was how to tune her carburetor or to sense when her tires were going bad. During Danica's first year of racing, T. J. had a hunch that racing was more than a hobby for Danica. He believed that his daughter had a gift.

Karting Star

Over a six-year period, the Patricks traveled countless weekends, six months a year, to kart races throughout the Midwest. Danica competed in about fifteen kart races a year. At the age of twelve, she won her first WKA national championship.

Sport doesn't discriminate about age, size or gender

<u>From the Pages of USA TODAY</u>

Who goes karting? Charlotte Motor Speedway President Humpy Wheeler did extensive research before inviting the World Karting Association to move to Charlotte [North Carolina]. He calls it "the largest underground sport in America today. No one knows really how many people are racing these things." The WKA and its sister group, the International Karting Federation, sanction [oversee] well over 1,000 races a year, but most races are non-sanctioned. This is one of the few sports where men and women compete on an equal basis. Cathy Hartman, according to IKF President Charles Cressi, "has won more karting events than anybody else," and Carolyn Andretti raced alongside brother John and cousins Michael and Jeff before choosing law school.

"Age means nothing to this sport," says Cressi. "You can always find a class that fits you. As a heavy person, you're not expected to compete against a light person." And 8-year-olds don't race against teen-agers.

George Kugler's trucking business kept him away from home a lot, so he took his sons racing as a way to spend time with them. Junior champion Robert Noaker Jr., 15, says his dad used to race karts but quit when "I was 2 or 3 . . . When I was 6, I asked for a race car and that's all it took." He found a four-cycle go-kart under the Christmas tree that year. The first few years, Noaker raced on a nearby dirt track at Hunterstown, Pa., with his dad as his crew chief. When he turned 11, he started racing enduro karts, too. Now, that's all he runs.

Noaker says he probably spends more time with his father than his two (older) sisters do, "but I think if we weren't doing this we'd find something else. We're real close." The family atmosphere that Edwin Davis values most about karting prevails. "It's real close. Everybody seems to help each other out."

—USA TODAY

In 1996, at the age of fourteen, Danica was accepted into the Lyn St. James Foundation Driver Development Program. Founded by Lyn St. James, the second woman ever to race in the Indy 500, the program helps young women enter the male-dominated sport of racing. At the academy in Indianapolis, Indiana, Danica learned about racing skills. But she also learned about the business side of the sport. Danica was trained to handle the media and learned how to approach sponsors.

Racing school: Lyn St. James *(right)* speaks to a group of Driver Development Program students in 2000.

That same year, Danica became a karting star. Of the forty-nine races she competed in, she won thirty-nine. In 1997 she took the WKA Grand National Championship title in two separate classes, the HPV class and Yamaha Lite class. Danica had proved to her opponents that she was a strong driver and fierce competitor. "Looking back," she later wrote, "I was probably a bigger bully than they were. I was really the one doing most of the intimidating."

IN FOCUS

The Extra Mile

Lyn St. James was with Danica during her first trip to the Indy 500—as a spectator. In 1997 St. James invited Danica to watch the race with her. St. James also took some time to introduce Danica to influential people in the world of racing, including potential sponsors. Although St. James spends a great deal of time and energy helping young women enter the sport of racing, she went the extra mile with Danica. "There's just another level that you're looking for with drivers," St. James has said. "She had an intensity that is unusual for someone that age."

Paving the way: Lyn St. James finishes a practice session in 2000. In 1992, she was the first woman to win the Indianapolis 500 Rookie of the Year award.

May 15, 1997

St. James driven to excel

From the Pages of
USA TODAY

Lyn St. James has had many memories. If she were the type who kept a scrapbook, it would bulge with reminders of "firsts," as in "the first woman" to accomplish this feat or break that barrier. That scrapbook would contain news clippings of her presence on the 1987 and '90 GTO teams that won the 24 Hours of Daytona. There would be news releases noting in 1985 she became the first woman to exceed 200 mph [322 km/h] on an oval, reaching 204.233 mph [328.7 km/h] in a Ford Mustang prototype at Talladega, Ala. And certainly photographs from 1992 of the standing ovation, led by four-time Indianapolis 500 champion A.J. Foyt, she received after being selected Indy Rookie of the Year.

Serving from 1990-93 as president of the Women's Sports Foundation, St. James decided through a namesake foundation to create a driver development program, targeting aspiring race-car drivers who are female, but open to both sexes.

Held in Indianapolis in November, the program brings in experts who counsel attendees in physical fitness, marketing, public speaking and the business of racing. Corporate board meetings, she points out, can be more bruising than what takes place on the track. For those older than 16, track time, with an emphasis on open-wheel driving, is included.

"The classes are small and aren't intended to change the world," she says, "but it does allow them to grab hold of something and think maybe they, too, can do with their life what they didn't before think was possible."

[One] graduate is Danica Patrick, 15, from Roscoe, Ill., the '96 World Karting Association Grand National champion. Patrick, who will compete this weekend in Canada, has her sights set on a Formula 2000 career when she turns 17 and legally is licensed. "I knew I could drive, but Lyn helped me see the importance of selling myself to sponsors and team owners," she says. "These days, being a great driver just isn't enough."

—Beth Tuschak

IN FOCUS

Early Rivalry

Sam Hornish Jr. won the 2006 Indy 500. He's also the first person to get into an accident with Danica. Like Danica, Sam's racing days began in karting. Sam and Danica were both entered in the 1994 WKA Grand National race. During the final lap, Danica was trailing Sam. To make a turn safely, Sam slowed down slightly by lifting his foot off the throttle (gas pedal). Danica, determined to win, continued to floor the throttle. She caught up to Sam and ran over his left rear tire. Danica's kart flipped and landed on top of Sam. The scene looked horrible, as if Sam and Danica were both seriously injured. Miraculously, both drivers walked away just fine.

Sam Hornish Jr.

Danica had performed extraordinarily well, and people began to notice. In 1997 Danica met John Mecom Jr., a Texas businessperson and former racing team owner. They talked about what it takes to move from karting to race car driving. Danica was excited to meet John Mecom, but she didn't think much of it. She was fifteen years old and a karting star. But she was also a young girl getting ready to start high school. Mecom, however, continued to watch Danica's performances on the track. Like Danica's father, Mecom had a hunch that

Danica had a gift. For the next two years, Mecom and his son John Mecam III followed Danica's karting career.

Life off the Track

While Danica was becoming a champion, she attended Hononegah Community High School in Rockton, Illinois. During the off-season, Danica had her weekends back and kept busy with normal high school activities. She dabbled in other sports, including softball and volleyball. She played flute and sang in the choir. She was also a cheerleader. And she had a job at Java Hut, her parents' coffee shop. But racing was her number one priority. Danica's passion for go-karts cost her a couple of high school activities. When she was in tenth grade, her cheerleading coach kicked her off the squad for missing too many games and practices. And her mother had to fire her from the Java Hut for showing up late too many times.

Off the squad: Danica *(bottom right)* wasn't always able to balance racing with other sports and activities.

The Next Level

During Danica's karting days, the Patricks got the family time they wanted. And Danica learned the value of family support. Her parents were always there to coach her and encourage a positive attitude. Her sister was her best friend, always cheering her on. Traveling together in a small pickup truck, family members had little private time on the weekends. But the bonds they created during this period would serve Danica many times in the years ahead.

Early on in her racing life, Danica would set goals. She would focus on reaching them and then surpassing them. She paid close attention to her movements while racing: what helped her to manage her speed, to handle turns more smoothly, and to maneuver her way through a pack of karts. For Danica, racing was more than a sport. It was her calling. If she were going to be the best in the world, she would have to dedicate herself to getting better.

At age sixteen, Danica sought more training. She wanted to take her driving skills to the next level—from a kart to a more powerful open-wheel race car. Like many other sixteen-year-old kids who work to earn a driver's license, Danica needed practice driving. Unlike her peers, she needed to practice moving in excess of 100 mph (161 km/h) if she wanted to try open-wheel racing.

 Some racing karts reach speeds of up to 80 miles per hour (129 km/h). They can go from 0 to 60 miles per hour (97 km/h) in about 3 seconds.

In 1999 Danica and her father visited the Mecoms to discuss the next level of training for Danica. The Mecoms agreed to sponsor Danica as she learned more about driving open-wheel cars. John Mecom III signed on as her manager for this period as well. But if the Mecoms were going to sponsor Danica, they wanted her to go to the best driving school.

The Mecoms led Danica and her family to an important decision—one that would affect Danica for years to come. At age sixteen, and with her family's support, Danica prepared to leave her home and family and even to drop out of high school. She was moving to Milton Keynes, England—the world's premier training ground for up-and-coming racers.

Danica's formal education ended in 1998, before she graduated from high school. Later, she passed the test to earn a General Education Degree (GED), which is the equivalent of a high school diploma.

Across the pond: Danica tests out an open-wheel car in November 1998, before her first season in England.

Driver's Training

■■■■

For T. J. and Bev, allowing Danica to move to England for more training was an easy decision. "If you want to be the best lawyer, you go to Harvard. If you want to be the best driver, you go to England," Bev said. T. J. couldn't imagine her not going. At the airport, the close-knit family said an emotional so-long, and Danica boarded her plane for the long flight across the Atlantic Ocean.

For Danica, going to England to learn how to drive race cars made sense. Since the age of ten, she knew what she wanted to do. She wanted to be a professional race car driver—and she wanted to be the best. Danica "never had a 'Plan B.'" She wasn't sure how exactly she'd reach her goal. But she did know a few things. She knew she needed to learn as much as she could about the sport, to practice, and to do it all with confidence. Danica went to England with a competitive spirit and six years of driving karts under her belt. Now she needed to learn all she could about open-wheel racing.

Watch and learn: Danica surveys a Formula One course in Silverstone, England, in 1998.

Motorsport Classes

Motorsports are divided into different groups. Indy Racing League (IRL), Formula One, and the National Association for Stock Car Auto Racing (NASCAR) are just a few of many motorsport classes. Each class makes its own rules, determines its own race locations and courses, and uses a specific type of vehicle. Some classes, such as NASCAR and IRL, have millions of fans. Other classes are less well-known but are important training grounds for young race car drivers. Some of these classes, known as developmental racing classes, help racers develop their skills. At age sixteen, Danica was ready to move from the WKA to a developmental racing series.

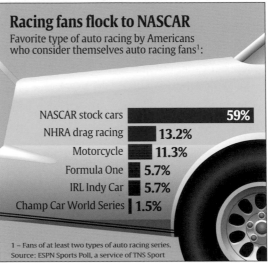

USA TODAY Snapshots®

Racing fans flock to NASCAR

Favorite type of auto racing by Americans who consider themselves auto racing fans[1]:

NASCAR stock cars	**59%**
NHRA drag racing	**13.2%**
Motorcycle	**11.3%**
Formula One	**5.7%**
IRL Indy Car	**5.7%**
Champ Car World Series	**1.5%**

1 – Fans of at least two types of auto racing series.
Source: ESPN Sports Poll, a service of TNS Sport

By Ellen J. Horrow and Frank Pompa, USA TODAY, 2004

The big leagues: NASCAR is one of the most popular sporting organizations in the United States.

Danica's goal was to eventually race in either the IRL or Formula One class. Both of these classes use open-wheel race cars. Like karts, the tires on an open-wheel car are exposed. Not covering them helps to make the car lighter and therefore faster. And just like a kart, open-wheel cars seat one person. Open-wheel cars are, however, larger and more powerful than karts. While karts can go around 80 miles per hour (129 km/h), some open-wheel cars reach speeds of 240 mph (386 km/h).

IN F CUS

Healthy Competition

IRL is part of a long, open-wheel racing history. It began with the Championship Auto Racing Teams (CART) class. In the 1990s, some people felt CART was adding too many road races (races that take place on large courses rather than oval tracks). They wanted to make sure racing continued on oval tracks as well. In 1994 CART became two separate leagues—Champ Car and IRL. The leagues competed for races, sponsors, and fans. Champ Car went bankrupt in 2004. In February of 2008, IRL and Champ Car merged once again under the IRL umbrella. Most people welcomed the merger and the healthy competition it would bring to the tracks.

Designed for speed: Indy race cars have exposed wheels for optimum speed.

Formula One was established in the United Kingdom in 1950. It is the most popular and glamorous class worldwide. It's not unusual for a Formula One team to spend more than two hundred million dollars on car development, testing, and engine improvements. The courses are 189 miles (304 km) long and include hairpin turns on narrow winding roads.

IRL is popular mostly in North America. But some drivers come

www.usatoday.com

● USA TODAY

Sports

SECTION C

June 25, 1992

Formula One racers face new regulations

<u>From the Pages of</u>
<u>USA TODAY</u>

The international governing body for motor sports, FISA [the French acronym for the International Federation of Car Racing], introduced measures Wednesday to make Formula One more competitive, including a mandatory tire change and a "safety car" to restart a race if there is an accident. The changes aim to breathe new life into Grand Prix racing, dominated during the past few years by Williams-Renault and McLaren-Honda teams.

One of the most radical changes: All cars must have at least four tires changed during a race. Another major change is the introduction, starting in July, of a safety car to neutralize a race in the event of a dangerous accident. The vehicle to be used in place of the traditional red flag will allow the race to restart, with competitors lining up behind the car. The car can be brought in at any time, starting with the third lap. Among technical regulations to be put in effect for 1993 is the reduction of the wheel and overall width of the car and a change in the size of the rear wing.

The FISA World Motor Council also asked that all measures be taken to introduce from outside the continent, and IRL races take place in several different countries, such as Japan. The IRL hosts the Indy 500, one of the biggest racing events in the United States. In the Indy 500, racers drive 200 laps around a 2.5-mile (4 km) oval track for a total of 500 miles (805 km). For Danica to reach either the IRL or a Formula One circuit, she would have to get some experience in a developmental racing series.

into Grand Prix racing unleaded non-toxic fuel, which is inexpensive and satisfies criteria for commercially available pump fuel. This would allow the smaller teams to be more competitive.

—Compiled by Ranald Totten

Safety first: A safety car *(with lights on top)* moves down the track at the Formula One Brazilian Grand Prix in Sao Paulo, Brazil, in 2003.

NASCAR is a motorsports class that races stock cars. Stock cars have basically the same frame as family sedans, and they handle much differently than open-wheel vehicles.

The Harvard of Racing Schools

The Formula Vauxhall Series is one of Britain's most distinguished developmental racing leagues. It's also one of the most competitive. Formula Vauxhall is run on a course of mostly winding roads. The series is a good opportunity for young racers, most of whom grew up racing karts, to try open-wheel racing. Formula Vauxhall cars reach speeds of up to 160 mph (257.50 km/h). Handling a car at such a high speed takes some practice. Danica was about to get some.

On the circuit, Danica was in heaven. She was sitting behind the

On the track: Racing open-wheel cars in England was a new thrill for Danica.

wheel of an open-wheel race car in England, a country known for taking racing seriously. Off the circuit, things were a little different.

Once again, Danica was the only female racing in the series. In Europe, racing is known for being even more male-dominated than it is in the United States. More than once, Danica heard team owners reprimanding a driver for losing to a girl. Danica, already accustomed to the attitude, did her best to put on her track face. But without the family support and encouragement Danica was used to, the attitudes of her peers felt sharper, more painful.

For the most part, Danica was on her own. After practice, the drivers hung out together. Most of the time,

Off the track: Danica *(above)* often felt isolated during her time in England.

they didn't invite Danica to come along. Before Danica left for England, her father had warned her about the dangers of experimenting with alcohol. But with the hope of fitting in, she started going to the pub, or bar, with some of her peers. "I thought I was old enough to make my own decisions," Danica would write later of her mind-set. "If I wanted to party, I would. Who would be there to check on me?" In England, Danica was of legal drinking age. Still, she knew it wasn't responsible.

She didn't drink and drive, but her focus did shift away from racing a bit. Like most teenagers, she wanted to belong.

Word of her drinking reached the Mecoms back in the States after the end of the 1998 Formula Vauxhall series, and they threatened to end their sponsorship. Suddenly, Danica

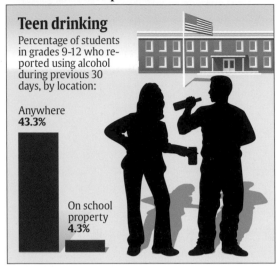

USA TODAY Snapshots®

Teen drinking

Percentage of students in grades 9-12 who reported using alcohol during previous 30 days, by location:

Anywhere
43.3%

On school property
4.3%

Source: Department of Education   By David Stuckey and Bob Laird, USA TODAY, 2007

was at risk of losing her place in the 1999 competition. Danica's sponsors and her family were paying a lot of money to advance her career. They needed her to take it as seriously as they were. Danica made one of the hardest phone calls of her life and pleaded with the Mecoms to continue their support.

Sponsoring a young driver on the developmental racing circuit in England can cost upwards of $150,000 a year.

After promising to clean up her act, Danica was given a second chance. She quit going to the pubs and made racing her number one priority. But she still faced obstacles. Although her sponsors were providing the owners of Danica's racing team with money for first-class equipment and crews, Danica felt that managers of the team weren't

Selling Skills

Racers are athletes, but they have to be salespeople as well. Drivers and racing teams work hard to get companies to pay for a team's expenses. In exchange, the drivers and the team advertise the sponsor's brand or product. Some sponsors contribute so much money that their name is part of the team's name. It's on the car and the driver's clothing. Other sponsors contribute smaller amounts. They might purchase a decal placed on the driver's helmet. Drivers and team owners take sponsorship seriously. If a driver is good enough, sponsors will come to his or her team. According to Danica, without sponsors she'd be "driving a cab."

spending the money on equipment for her. Male racers, it seemed, were getting the equipment slated for Danica. Still, Danica worked with what she had.

Formula Ford Festival

After racing just part of the Formula Vauxhall Winter Series in 1998, Danica raced the full 1999 season. This time around, she also received some financial support from the Ford Motor Company. That year she came in ninth place in the overall standings, an awesome finish for a seventeen-year-old. Racing officials in Europe began to take notice of this petite American girl. In 2000 Danica stepped up to the more prestigious Formula Ford series as part of the competitive Haywood Racing team. The biggest event for this series is the Formula Ford Festival. Danica wowed spectators when she wove through the course, passing drivers left and right, to cross the finish line one-half second later than the first-place winner. Danica's second-place finish was the highest ever for a female driver in the history of the Formula

Record finish: Danica *(on the course, above, and celebrating, below)* took second place at the 2000 Formula Ford Festival in Brands Hatch, England.

Ford Festival. She also tied with Danny Sullivan for the highest-ever finish by an American. Sullivan came in second place in 1974.

Danica had used another Haywood teammate's old chassis (the frame of a car) during the race. Her performance made her less sure about her racing team's level of support. "What I discovered after that race was that up to this point, I hadn't been given the opportunity to drive the right cars," Danica later wrote. "Despite the second-hand vehicle, it was better than any car I had driven during my first couple of years abroad."

 Some open-wheel cars reach speeds of 240 mph (386 km/h). Cars used in developmental classes aren't as fast, but they can reach speeds of around 124 mph (200 km/h).

Two of the spectators Danica wowed were her old coach Lyn St. James and former Indy racer Bobby Rahal. Rahal was working in England at the same time Danica was racing the developmental series there. St. James and Rahal talked about Danica's skill and potential. Rahal had already noticed her abilities. He also recognized that leaving home to race in England proved she was dedicated to the sport. Rahal, who has described England's developmental series as "the motor racing equivalent of a street fight," was impressed.

Racing legend: Former Indy racer Bobby Rahal noticed Danica's talent early on. Rahal won the Indy 500 in 1986 and joined the International Motorsports Hall of Fame in 1994.

May 26, 2006

Driving talent found in all states, levels

From the Pages of
USA TODAY

When it comes to discovering talent in stick and ball sports, it's relatively easy. Future hoops stars can be found at AAU [Amateur Athletic Union] basketball camps and high school gyms. Major League Baseball hopefuls are groomed in colleges and the minor leagues. When it comes to locating the next generation of Jeff Gordons [Daytona 500-winning NASCAR driver], the business is a lot trickier. There are so many different places a race car driver can get started, so many racetracks and so many routes to take. Should a driver race in midgets, sprints or go-karts? On road courses or ovals?

In auto racing, there is no clear-cut path to the top. Even though some team owners have tried to create a system to uncover hidden talent, there are no scouting departments. Most drivers are still plucked from small-town tracks because they somehow were able to grab the attention of someone important.

"It's like looking for that needle in the haystack," says Dan Davis, Ford's director of racing technology. In a typical year, Davis estimates that he will attend about 40 races. "I don't ever go to a race just to look for young talent," Davis says. "But there's so much sponsor money now that you can't afford to have someone in your seat who's almost good enough. If you're not winning, the sponsor wants to move on."

Even if talent is discovered, there are a slew of other intangibles that must also be double-checked before a team and sponsor are going to take a risk on that driver. Teams look at winning but also at marketability. Will the driver produce good quotes for the media and thereby grab free publicity for sponsors? Teams also want to make sure a driver can win even if the equipment isn't at its best.

Getting more women involved in racing is something in which Ford has taken an interest. And now it has a major sponsor, Clorox, involved as well. "We're trying to produce a Cup-winning female driver," Davis says. "And we wanted Clorox to understand that this was going to be a long-term commitment." Danica Patrick made a splash at the Indy 500 last year and nearly won the race. This season another woman is making her mark in open-wheel racing as well: Katherine Legge. She is in her first season in the Champ Car World Series. At the start of the season, she only had a contract to race half of the races, but she won three times, earning her a full-time ride.

—Amy Rosewater

In 2001 Danica continued to race in England, but with fewer strong finishes. The Ford Motor Company, the Mecoms, and Danica herself still felt that the managers at Haywood Racing were not spending her sponsorship money properly. Although they often promised to give Danica better equipment, they rarely followed through. And the Mecoms, who were located overseas, found it difficult to fight on her behalf. Not getting an even break was a constant source of frustration for Danica during her time in England. After a while, Ford ended its sponsorship, and Danica had the chance to drive in only five Formula Ford races. But the end couldn't have come at a better time. Danica had proved she could handle an open-wheel race car with the best of them. She was ready to go home.

Back in the States: After her training period in England ended, Danica went looking for sponsors.

Start Your Engines!

Danica was happy to be home, surrounded by friends and family once again. The negative attitudes she faced in England left her stronger than she was when she first left the States. If anything, Danica was even more competitive.

Danica had proved she could race an open-wheel car. Now it was time to find a job. To be part of a team, it would help to have a sponsor. Getting the attention of people in the racing world meant hanging out at the garages of racetracks, talking to sponsors, team owners, or whoever would listen. Danica's father (T. J.) was once again at her side. The two of them hit the road looking for opportunities. At first, the Patricks met rejection after rejection. Danica was disappointed but remained hopeful. She knew she'd find a team. She had no doubt. It was only a matter of time.

Bobby Rahal and Danica had met a few times during Danica's stay in England. Rahal remembered Danica's performances and admired her grit. He arranged a tryout for Danica with Tom Milner, the owner of Prototype Technology Group (PTG). PTG is an organization that tests new car technology and races in multiple classes. Danica briefly joined PTG and became a paid professional driver for the first time. But Danica was never able to race the cars that Milner hired her to drive. The series for which they were made came out with unexpected new rules, and PTG's cars were suddenly ineligible. It was another false start.

Before every race, drivers must go through qualifying rounds. Racers drive the course alone, without other vehicles on the track. The fastest drivers are allowed to enter the race. The fastest driver is given the pole position: the first, and most favored, starting position on the track. The driver who earns the pole position is called the pole-sitter. In most races, drivers earn money for becoming a pole-sitter.

In April 2002, Danica participated in the Toyota Pro/Celebrity Race. The race is a fund-raiser that takes place in Long Beach, California. Celebrities buy a chance to race in the event. The money goes to help children's hospitals in southern California. The race is meant to be fun. But all drivers, whether celebrity or professional, still take it seriously. Drivers go ten laps around a 1.97-mile (3.17 km) road course. At the end of the race, Danica made headlines. She and Dara Torres became the first women ever to win the race. Dara Torres, a swimmer and nine-time Olympic medalist, won overall and in the celebrity category. Danica won in the professional category. The fund-raiser was fun, but Danica's sights were still set on Formula or IRL racing.

First female winners: Swimmer Dara Torres *(left)* won overall while Danica won in the pro category at the 2002 Toyota Pro/Celebrity Race in Long Beach, California.

All for One and One for All

In most motorsport classes, racers belong to a team. Every team has one or more owners, cars, pit crews, engineers, spotters, race car drivers, and sponsors. Each team usually has three drivers, all of whom compete in the same race. By having more than one driver in the race, the team owner increases the team's chances of winning. A team's drivers race against other teams. They also race against each other. Drivers have their own pit crews and other support people. In any open-wheel pit crew, there are about twenty different mechanics. This includes eight people responsible for carrying tires! Four workers take off old tires, and another four people put new tires in place.

It's a Deal

Danica had been able to drive at Long Beach with the help of Bobby Rahal, who gave her a spot in the race. After Danica's Toyota Pro/Celebrity Race win, Rahal took on the task of arranging most of her test-drives and tracked her progress. Eventually, he contacted Danica with an offer to be part of the team.

"Signing Danica as a driver was an easy decision for me," Rahal later said. "Her talent was obvious. Her commitment is what really spoke to me."

Rahal, along with television host David Letterman, owned Team Rahal Racing (which later became Rahal Letterman Racing). The team raced in the IRL. But before Rahal would let Danica race the Indy 500, he wanted her to get more practice. During her three years in England, Danica had been driving Formula cars on road courses. The switch from Formula to IRL meant she'd be driving on some oval tracks. Danica needed to get used to driving in circles again, like she had done during her karting days.

Robert "Bobby" Rahal raced professionally from 1982 to 1998. Rahal won twenty-four open-wheel races in the CART series, including the 1986 Indy 500. He also won championship titles in 1986, 1987, and in 1992.

Rahal entered Danica in the Barber Dodge Pro Series, an entry level open-wheel racing series. She made her Pro Series debut in Toronto, Ontario, Canada, on July 7, 2002, and finished seventh in her first race. Danica competed in five events total throughout the series, with a best finish of fourth place. Then, in 2003, she advanced to the Toyota Atlantic Championship Series—the top developmental open-wheel racing series in the United States.

Pro Series: Bobby Rahal *(left)* checks in with Danica before the 2002 Molson Indy Vancouver race in Vancouver, Canada.

February 14, 1996

Letterman joins Rahal IndyCar team as an owner

<u>From the Pages of USA TODAY</u>

David Letterman doesn't have a top-10 list of reasons for deciding to invest in a racing team. He offers just one: a lifelong love of the sport. The late-night talk show host was formally introduced Tuesday as a minority owner in Bobby Rahal's IndyCar team.

"This has been in me since I was a kid. I've been in love with racing and its heroes for as long as I can remember," said Letterman, an Indianapolis native. "I don't want this perceived as Mr. Big Shot TV Guy coming into something he doesn't know anything about." No other reason for getting involved? "I get to drive when Bobby's playing golf," he said.

Rahal, 43, who fields Mercedes-powered Reynards for himself and Bryan Herta, split with partner Carl Hogan after last season. The three-time IndyCar champ, trying to end a three-year winless streak, says he and Letterman have talked casually about forming a partnership since they met in 1986.

"We agreed if the time was ever right, we'd give it serious consideration," he said. "With my starting the new team, it finally seemed to make sense." Letterman said he will be as involved as possible "without getting in people's way," but he will be limited in the number of events he can attend. "I do have another job," he reminded.

—Steve Ballard

New interest: David Letterman watches preparations for the 2005 Indy 500.

Toyota Atlantic Championship Series

Before the 2003 season even started, Danica was making headlines. In 2003 she became the first woman in the Toyota Atlantic Championship Series' thirty-year history to race full-time. Rahal went to great lengths to get Danica on the track. He created a team specifically for her.

Danica's first race was the Tecate/Telmex Monterrey Grand Prix, held in Monterrey, Mexico. During qualifying rounds, she came in fifth

www.usatoday.com

USA TODAY

Sports

SECTION C

March 19, 2003

Photogenic Patrick one of guys on track

From the Pages of **USA TODAY**   Danica Patrick wants to be known as just a race car driver rather than a female driver, but that hasn't stopped her from capitalizing on the difference. Patrick, who turns 21 Tuesday, is using her photogenic looks to attract attention to her entry in the CART Toyota Atlantic Championship, a training series for major open-wheel racing. She doesn't mind flaunting that image if it helps raise backing to achieve her goal of competing in the CART Champ Car World Series and the Indianapolis 500.

"Eventually I hope to lose it, but I'm going to use it to my full advantage, just like anybody else would who has a niche," Patrick says. "At the end of the day, when I take the helmet off, I'm still a girl."

Patrick is being groomed for open-wheel stardom by former CART champion and Indy 500 winner Bobby Rahal, a car owner in CART and the IRL. "I think she has the potential to get to the top," Rahal says. "I think she's the first woman who truly has the race-craft to succeed."

place out of fifteen drivers. She finished the race in third place, becoming the first woman to earn a podium (top three) finish. Danica entered twelve races that season. She finished in the top five four times and crashed twice, taking her out of the race both times. At the Argent Mortgage Toyota Atlantic 100k in Cleveland, Ohio, the final race of the season, Danica took second place. Overall, she had a good season, finishing in the top five of the fifteen drivers.

Patrick cut her auto racing teeth in the cutthroat competition of British road racing, starting when she was 16. Her best result was runner-up in the 2000 British Formula Ford Festival. She won last year's Toyota Pro Celebrity race at the Long Beach Grand Prix [in Long Beach, California], beating former Trans-Am champion Tommy Kendall and IndyCar fan favorite Sarah Fisher. Patrick is determined to become known and successful because of her ability rather than her gender.

"I'm very serious about every aspect of fitness," Patrick says. "When people look at me, they think, 'You're just a little thing.' When they shake my hand, they say, 'OK, you're tough.' Then they'll see me out on the track and realize that I can handle the race with as much power as the next guy."

— Mark Fogarty

All dressed up: Danica attends the GQ Men of the Year Awards in 2003.

Tecate/Telmex Grand Prix: Danica's first Toyota Atlantic Championship race was held in Monterrey, Mexico. She came in third, while Jonathan Macri *(left)* took second palce and Michael Valiante *(middle)* took first.

In 2004 Danica once again competed in the Toyota Atlantic Championship Series. The fifth race of the season was held in Portland, Oregon. Danica earned the pole position during qualifying rounds, making her the first female driver to win a Toyota Atlantic pole position. Her lead ended during the first lap of the race, though, when

IN FOCUS

The Point System

Drivers are always interested in winning a race. But they're also interested in scoring points. Each racing league has its own point system. In the IRL, racers earn fifty points for coming in first place. Racers who follow earn fewer points. In addition, whoever leads the most laps earns two points. And, the pole-sitter gets an additional one point. At the end of the season, whoever has the most points is the season's champion driver.

another driver hit her from behind. Neither she nor her car was seriously damaged. But the time spent repairing the vehicle led to a seventh-place finish.

Ready for takeoff: Josh Hunt's car tumbles in front of Danica during the eighth race of the 2004 season.

Danica finished the season in third place overall, a respectable feat. She hadn't won a race, but she did win the confidence of Bobby Rahal. In December 2004, Rahal announced that in 2005 Danica would move up to the Indy Racing League. Rahal slated her for all seventeen IRL races in the IndyCar Series. The IndyCar Series is the IRL's premier racing series, and it includes the Indy 500. Danica's dreams were coming true.

Indy cars are the fastest race cars and can reach speeds of up to 240 miles per hour (386 km/h). Small and lightweight, the vehicles are built to minimize drag, or air resistance. Like karts, Indy cars are open-wheel vehicles, meaning the tires are completely exposed.

In the IRL: Danica charges down Florida's Homestead-Miami Speedway in 2005.

The Rookie

■■■■■

As a kid, Danica had the same scary dream over and over again: she was being chased by wolves. As fast as she ran, she couldn't escape. Her dream ended with her being unable to scream or even move. During the 2005 IRL season, Danica overcame her fear. "I'm no longer terrified of being chased," wrote Danica in her autobiography. "It [means I'm] in the lead."

Danica had won only one race since her karting days. Now that she was in the IRL, she was ready to prove she could compete in the big league. Her strategy was the same. Practice, learn, focus, and be confident. She continued to follow her father's advice. Each time she went on the track, Danica made a point to learn something. She would use her rookie year in the IRL to learn from her mistakes—and to set some records.

IN FOCUS

The IRL Point System

The IRL awards points to a driver based on where he or she finishes a race. As of 2009, extra points are also awarded to the driver who leads the most laps and the driver who claims a race's pole position. These points add up over the course of a season, and eventually determine where a driver places overall. Points are awarded for every IRL race using the same system:

Position	Points
1st	50
2nd	40
3rd	35
4th	32
5th	30
6th	28
7th	26
8th	24
9th	22
10th	20
11th	19
12th	18
13th	17
14th	16
15th	15
16th	14
17th	13
18th	12
19th	12
20th	12
21st	12
22nd	12
23rd	12
24th	12
25th	10
26th	10
27th	10
28th	10
29th	10
30th	10
31st	10
32nd	10
33rd	10

A Rough Start

Danica's rookie season started out with a bang—and a head injury. During lap 158 of the Toyota Indy 300 in Miami, the first race of the season, Danica was involved in an eight-car accident. She suffered a concussion and wasn't able to finish the race. But two weeks later, after receiving some advanced therapy for her injury, she was back on the track in Phoenix, Arizona, where she placed fifteenth. Her third race ended with a disappointing twelfth-place finish. During her fourth race, which took place in Motegi, Japan, she started second and led for thirty-two laps before finishing fourth. Things were starting to look up for Danica. And it was a good thing. The Indy 500, the race Danica had dreamed about since she was a kid, was next on the schedule.

Accident: Eight drivers including Tomas Scheckter *(upper left)*, Koseuke Matsuura *(right)*, and Scott Sharp *(second from right)* crashed during the first race of the 2005 IRL season at Homestead-Miami Speedway in Homestead, Florida. Danica also crashed while trying to avoid the accident.

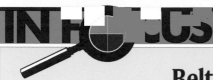

Belting In

Open-wheel drivers buckle up with six safety belts. The belts are strapped tight over the shoulders and lap and through the legs. The belts are so tight that the driver can't move around. The driver sits with hands on the wheel, legs extended in the nose (front end) of the car, and torso (upper body) leaning backward slightly. During the Indy 500, racers stay in this position for two to four hours straight. But maintaining this rigid position is worth it. If the driver gets into a high-speed crash, he or she has a smaller chance of getting injured. And by releasing only one buckle, drivers can easily free themselves.

For Danica, being safe involves "a constant state of excruciating pain and discomfort." Because she is short, the car's safety belts go directly over her hip bones and "feel like knives digging into [her] hips." Adding padding is not an option because it creates extra wiggle room.

Buckle up: A pit crew member adjusts one of Danica's six safety belts.

Getting Ready

The Indy 500 takes place during Memorial Day weekend, on the last Sunday of the month of May. Every year, about 350,000 fans crowd the bleachers at the Indianapolis Motor Speedway, also known as the Brickyard. Regulars at the Brickyard have ear muffs handy. They know they're going to need them when the drivers start to rev their engines.

The Indianapolis Motor Speedway is nicknamed "the Brickyard." The 2.5-mile (4 km) track was formerly paved with 3.2 million bricks. Over the years, workers have covered the Brickyard with asphalt. Only a 36-inch (1 meter) strip of the original brick is still visible at the starting line.

Crowd-pleaser: Nearly four hundred thousand people travel to the Indianapolis Motor Speedway to watch the Indianapolis 500 each year.

At the 2005 Indy 500, the spectators were excited for the biggest race of the year. Danica Patrick was starting in fourth place, the highest-ever start for a woman in the Indy 500. Before getting in the car, Danica and her crew double-checked to make sure everything was in order. Danica said a prayer with her family and the track chaplain. She put on her helmet, got in car number sixteen, and buckled up.

The Restart of the Century

Going into the 2005 Indy 500, Danica and her crew had a strategy planned out. But the events of the race called for some fast thinking.

At lap 57, Danica took her now historic first-place lead. By lap 79, Danica had dropped to third place. She had been driving hard, taking only 25 seconds to complete a lap. Danica made a pit stop to refuel and change tires. But on her way out she held the clutch and stalled. The mistake cost her precious seconds. She returned to the track in sixteenth place.

Pit stop: Danica's crew changes her tires and fills up her fuel cell at the 2005 Indy 500 in Indianapolis, Indiana.

Gearing Up

Racing is a dangerous sport. Drivers use some advanced technology to stay safe. High-speed crashes can sometimes end in flames, so all of a racer's clothing is fireproof. Socks, gloves, underwear, balaclava (head cover), and racing suit are made of Nomex, a material that NASA developed in the 1960s for astronauts.

Every IRL helmet comes with built-in earplugs, speakers, and a microphone. The earplugs protect the

Head to toe: Danica's racing gear is fireproof, from her socks to her head cover.

Tunnel vision: Danica can see only what's directly in front of her when she wears a safety helmet.

driver's hearing. The loud rumble of the race car engines and the hollow roar of fast-moving vehicles as they circle the track produce a deafening sound. Helmets also help drivers to see. When driving on the track, racers can view only what's directly in front of them. They have no peripheral, or side, vision. To know whether a car is passing on the left or right, racers rely on a spotter. Spotters are crew members who stand perched above the track. They use a microphone and speakers to notify their racer when another car is about to pass. Drivers hear the messages through speakers,

which are implanted in their earplugs. The driver's microphone is tucked into the helmet's chin padding.

Between the Nomex suit, the heat of the engine, and outdoor temperatures, drivers can get super hot. They sweat a lot during the entire race and risk getting dehydrated, or losing too much body fluid. To keep hydrated, racers drink water through a small plastic tube that is fed through a hole in their helmets. They pull the balaclava from over their mouth, bite on the tube, and press a button on the steering wheel to get the water flowing.

About three-quarters of the way through the race, the race marshal waved a yellow flag. A yellow flag means caution; all drivers must
maintain a slow and steady pace. During a yellow flag, racers are not
allowed to pass one another. Danica was in ninth place. During lap
155, the marshal lifted the yellow flag and the racers were off again.
Danica pressed hard on the throttle, causing her car to do a quarter
spin. The nosecone (front end) hit two other cars. Danica needed to
make a pit stop for repairs. The two other drivers were out of the race.
Once again, Danica was in sixteenth place.

Damage control: An accident midway through the 2005 Indy 500 forced Danica
to stop for repairs.

Shortly after the 2005 Indy 500, Danica auctioned
off the damaged nosecone of her number sixteen
car. It sold for more than two thousand dollars. The
money went to charity.

In the lead: Danica nudges ahead of competitor Dan Wheldon *(far left)* during the 2005 Indy 500.

In lap 182, Danica's number sixteen car once again took the lead. Her team made a decision: no more pit stops. Danica would have to complete the race with the fuel remaining in the car's cell, or tank. Four laps later, racer Dan Wheldon passed Danica. Then a yellow flag appeared, and all cars had to slow down. For Danica, this was good news. Slowing down meant she was conserving fuel. In second place, she would have to do what she could to return to the lead. Through the microphone in her helmet, she heard her engineer Ray Leto's voice. "Danica, we need the restart of the twenty-first century."

Danica responded. The marshal lifted the yellow flag and Danica peeled off, regaining the lead for four laps. Although Danica led eighteen of the last twenty-eight laps in the race, she couldn't hold the lead until the end. Wheldon and other lead drivers had fresh tires and fuel. One by one they passed her. She finished the race in fourth place and took home almost 380,000 dollars in prize money. A couple of mistakes and the need to conserve fuel most likely cost her a victory.

June 24, 2005

Can you identify this man?
Indy 500 champ Wheldon
quietly makes spectacular rise

<u>From the Pages of</u>
<u>USA TODAY</u>

When Dan Wheldon returns home to England and tries to buy a pint of ale at the corner pub, some grateful bloke [guy] will surely recognize the first Brit to win the Indianapolis 500 since 1966. But unless Wheldon is near his St. Petersburg, Fla., home, he can probably walk anywhere in the USA without being recognized as the winner of the "Greatest Spectacle in Racing."

Wheldon couldn't care less about his fame because life on the track is too sweet. The defending champion in Saturday night's SunTrust Indy Challenge in Richmond,

Moving into first: Dan Wheldon *(right)* passes Danica on lap 194 of the 2005 Indy 500. Wheldon would stay in the lead for the last six laps for the win.

Va., has four wins in six IRL Indy-Car Series starts. Being off to the best start in IRL history could also help Wheldon become the first driver to win Indy and the title in the same year.

"When I started the season, my goal wasn't the championship, it was the 500," says Wheldon, who turned 27 Wednesday. "I don't get hyped up about the statistics, but I don't want to win the championship just on being consistent. I want to win it with a lot of race wins," Wheldon says.

Danica Patrick, whose historic fourth-place finish at Indy has made her a media magnet, earned a *Sports Illustrated* cover after that race. Yet Wheldon hasn't felt bitter. He knows Patrick's talent and looks have increased awareness for the IRL and believes everybody will benefit by that. Over the long run he also believes the public will remember his achievement—especially back home.

"I really don't care what people think because I wanted to win that race for a long time and I'll always have that," Wheldon says.

Still, Wheldon's second-fiddle status has become a running joke among drivers. At Texas he sported a T-shirt reading "Actually Won The Indy 500" provided by Buddy Rice, who wore a shirt saying "Danica's teammate."

Indy tradition: Dan Wheldon drinks the traditional milk after winning the Indy 500 in 2005. After winning the Indy 500 in 1936, racer Louis Meyer asked for a glass of buttermilk. From that day forward, almost every Indy winner has drunk a glass or pint of milk at the end of the race. To keep the tradition going, the American Dairy Association pays winners $10,000 to drink the beverage.

—Gary Graves

Fame and Fortune

Just being entered in the 2005 Indy 500 was a source of great joy for Danica. She was thrilled to drive at the Brickyard. Even though Danica didn't win the race, the record she set took her career to a new level. From that point onward, Danica Patrick was no longer seen as just another racer. She was a household name. Even people who weren't interested in Indy racing had heard of Danica Patrick, the female racer who led nineteen laps and finished fourth in the 2005 Indy 500.

Danica's fans wanted to know everything about her. She responded by giving dozens of television, radio, and newspaper interviews.

IN FOCUS

Ways to Win

Crossing the finish line first sometimes requires drivers to go slower than their opponents. Driving at a slower speed conserves fuel. An IndyCar has a 40-gallon (151 liters) fuel cell, or tank. When driving more than 200 miles per hour (322 km/h), IndyCars burn about one gallon (3.78 liters) of ethanol every 30 seconds. Having to refuel at the wrong time—when the driver is in the lead at the end of a race, for instance—can cost the team the race. One way to save fuel is to draft. Drafting is riding directly behind another car. This reduces air resistance so the driver can let up slightly on the throttle. When the driver lets up on the throttle, he or she is saving fuel.

Getting through pit stops quickly is also important. While Danica is driving around the track, a computer in her car delivers information about her car's performance to a computer located at the pit stop. The team engineer, who's also at the pit stop, reviews the information. When Danica makes a pit stop, her crew must change tires, refuel, clear debris from the car, and make adjustments based on the computer's feedback all within fifteen seconds. To win, Danica depends on her skills and on her fast and dedicated crew.

May 31, 2005

Girl, uninterrupted

<u>From the Pages of USA TODAY</u>

Danica Patrick shattered several records Sunday at the storied Indianapolis 500. Even more lasting will be the point she made. In a car hitting 226 miles an hour [364 km/h], Patrick, 23, was the first woman to hold the lead at any time in the race's 89-year history. Her fourth place finish was the best ever for a woman. She also proved a point that won't be in the record books, but should be: A woman with the right talent can succeed in a male-dominated sport such as auto racing when she's given the right backing from people who take her seriously.

Patrick's dad, T.J. Patrick, a championship snowmobile racer, did just that when Danica and her younger sister got into go-kart racing as kids. T.J. didn't treat them as girls. Janet Guthrie, the first woman to race at Indy, in 1977, recalls in her memoirs being told by an auto executive that she would never win because "no one will ever give you a winning car because you are a woman." The dismal prediction proved accurate, she says.

Patrick's ride changed all that. Racing legend Bobby Rahal saw her potential and signed her in 2002 to join his top-flight team. This year, Patrick almost took it all before the ultimate winner, Dan Wheldon, 26, passed her with seven laps to go. Asked whether he was focused on passing Patrick, Indy's big story all last week, Wheldon replied that he wasn't "looking at it like it was Danica Patrick. It was just another Rahal car." Now that's real progress.

—USA TODAY's editors

Proud papa: T. J. Patrick congratulates Danica after the 2005 Indy 500.

Much of the attention had to do with the fact that Danica did so well in the race as a woman. Headlines such as "Meet the Fastest Female in Indy 500," "Danica Patrick Gives the Indy 500 Sex Appeal," "Brit Edges Woman to Win Indy," and "Woman Makes History at Indy 500 without Checkered Flag" splashed across newspapers, magazines, and web pages worldwide. Even Dan Wheldon, the winner of the race, received far less media attention. But for Danica, focusing on her gender seemed ridiculous. After all, her performance proved that racing is a level playing

May 26, 1989

Sponsorship goes to racers' heads

<u>From the Pages of</u>
<u>USA TODAY</u>

For some, the roughest competition at the Indy 500 doesn't start until after the checkered flag waves. That's when they begin the Hat Dance, a victory lane ritual peculiar to auto racing. This is where the representatives of corporate America do battle to make sure the winner is photographed wearing a hat that bears their company logo. It doesn't matter that the winning driver has just spent three hours in 100-degree [38 degrees Celsius] heat. He's not going anywhere until payback time is finished for the people who have been paying the bills. And it can get nasty. Like if a car with GM Goodwrench parts wins a race run by the Motorcraft people who make Ford parts.

No one is certain who [is responsible for the Hat Dance tradition], but many credit retired Goodyear man Mike Babich. In the late '60s he went to his boss and said he was going to stick a much larger company logo on a hat, and get it on the head of field for men and women. "My car has no idea if I am male or female," Danica would later write. But the focus on Danica's gender continued.

Highlights

For Danica, 2005 will always stand out as a memorable year. She finished twelfth overall in the IRL points standings that year. She was named 2005 Bombardier Rookie of the Year by the Bombadier Learjet company, Indy 500 Rookie of the Year, and *USA Today* and U.S. Sports

a winner. "He said he thought it was obscene to put on the big patch," says Babich. "Things were a little more subtle in those days."

One of the most experienced Hat Men is Bill Brodrick, a Unical press spokesman who for 20 years has been given the responsibility of sorting out victory lane chaos at tracks all over the country. "It's a pretty simple formula," says Brodrick. "The people who spend the most get there first."

Sometimes it's not just the sponsors who are on edge. One year David Pearson won the grueling Rockingham 500 and found himself doing the Hat Dance when what he really needed was a trip to the restroom. "He was miserable," says Brodrick. "Finally, he ran out. He yelled 'I'm done.'"

The unwritten rule is that the car's sponsor gets first shot, followed by the race sponsor, and then all the associate sponsors and manufacturers. But when something unforseeable disrupts the process, like with Pearson's bladder, there are serious ramifications.

"There are a lot of folks, myself included, who have been raked over the coals because the hats weren't on at a certain time," says Steve Jones, a former Coors P.R. man who now is president of his sports marketing company. "Probably the most physical I've seen it was at Pocono, Pa., last year, when one of the auto manufacturing reps was literally carried out of victory lane by track security, when he simply was in there trying to make certain his sponsors' hats were on at the appointed time."

—Tom Weir

Fan favorite: Danica's 2005 Indy 500 performance grabbed the attention of racing fans nationwide.

Academy Female Athlete of the Year. She appeared on *The Late Show with David Letterman*, *The Today Show*, ESPN, CNN, *Good Morning America*, and more.

But if you ask Danica, she might say her biggest day of the year was November 19, 2005. On that day, Danica married Paul Hospenthal, her physical therapist since 2001. Danica and Paul first met after Danica pulled a hip muscle while doing yoga. She soon found herself calling him whenever she was near Phoenix, Arizona, where Paul lived and worked. According to Danica, Paul is a private person, and he was originally cautious about entering a relationship with such a high-profile person. But, "the more he tried to convince himself that this was wrong, the more he became convinced that it was right."

These days, Paul does not seem to be bothered by Danica's celebrity status. According to Danica, Paul offers his unwavering support: "I have his whole heart and he has mine," she says. He clears his schedule to attend her races, encourages Danica to keep her expectations high, and is a model of patience and tolerance. "Paul's presence added to my race experience," Danica claims. "I found myself calmer and more relaxed before a race."

Good match: Danica and her husband, Paul Hospenthal, leave the Indianapolis Motor Speedway after the exhausting 2005 race.

Getting focused: Danica prepares for a practice lap at the Nashville Superspeedway in Nashville, Tennessee.

Moving Forward

Over the years, the IRL had been becoming less and less popular with racing fans compared to NASCAR. More people, it seemed, were interested in watching NASCAR's Coca-Cola 600 than the Indy 500. This race airs after the Indy 500 on Memorial Day weekend. In 2005 Danica changed all that. For the first time in years, the Indy 500 had more TV viewers than the Coca-Cola 600.

Whether IRL drivers liked racing with a woman or not, they were beginning to realize something important. Danica was not only a strong competitor. She was good for the sport. Singlehandedly, Danica drew thousands of viewers to the Indy 500. Media coverage followed. The more attention Danica got, the more attention the IRL got.

IN FOCUS

When Tempers Flare

Danica is passionate about racing. If she feels other racers are bad sports, she lets them know. In 2007 in Milwaukee, Wisconsin, Danica was passing Dan Wheldon when their cars touched. The impact forced her car into the infield. Danica was able to regain control of her car, but it needed repairs. Wheldon finished in third place, and Danica finished eighth. Afterward, Danica gave Wheldon a piece of her mind—and a light push to go along with it. She believed Wheldon bumped into her on purpose so she wouldn't be able to pass. Neither driver was penalized for their behavior. Sports officials considered it a normal racing incident.

Book Deal

In January 2006, Danica Mania was going strong. Danica contracted with Simon & Schuster, a publishing company, to write her life story. The publisher wanted Danica to write about her experiences, so people could see how she was able to achieve so much in such a short period of time. Newspaper and magazine articles informed fans about Danica's achievements. But the people at Simon & Schuster hoped that a book would tell the whole story. Racing season begins every year in March. The book had to be on the shelves before the 2006 Indy 500 in May. Danica got to work, writing whenever she had a spare moment. She collaborated on the project with Laura Morton, an author who had helped other celebrities tell their stories.

The book, called *Danica: Crossing the Line*, came out on schedule. Readers had mixed reactions to the autobiography. Some readers were inspired by the challenges Danica had to overcome as a female racer.

Danica the author: Danica holds up a copy of her autobiography at a book signing in 2006.

Others were disappointed. They felt that Danica wrote too much about her talent and drive for success. Regardless of the split opinions, it was another achievement for Danica. At age twenty-three, she already had enough material to fill 200 pages.

Back to Racing

The 2006 IRL season found Danica and her teammates in the news again—but with little to celebrate. Danica's 2006 teammates on Rahal Letterman Racing were Buddy Rice and Paul Dana. During a practice session for the first race at Homestead-Miami Speedway, Paul Dana was killed when he crashed into the back of a stalled race car. Bobby Rahal, Danica, and Buddy were devastated.

IN FOCUS

Accidents

Car racing is a dangerous sport. Since the early 1900s, more than three hundred drivers worldwide have lost their lives racing professionally. Drivers aren't the only people at risk of getting hurt at a motorsports event. At the Brickyard alone, more than sixty people have lost their lives, many of them spectators or mechanics as well as drivers.

Racing officials have done a lot over the years to improve safety conditions for drivers, crews, and spectators. Still, at every Indy 500 race, about two hundred fifty medical professionals and more than twenty ambulances are on hand to treat injuries. They are also available to help anyone who may be suffering from a medical condition, such as a heart attack or stroke. Almost every professional track also has a track chaplain. It's not uncommon to see drivers and their families saying a prayer with the chaplain before a race.

Lost friend: On March 26, 2006, a crash took the life of driver Paul Dana.

Rahal immediately pulled Danica and Buddy from the race. It was a hard decision to make. Taking them out of the race meant they wouldn't earn any points that day, putting them at a disadvantage for the entire season. But it was the right thing to do. Danica and Buddy might not be concentrating fully, Rahal thought. He needed them to be in top shape, physically and mentally. Race car drivers are well aware that serious accidents and death are always a possibility in their job. Although the drivers that day were prepared to carry on, the mood was somber. Rahal told reporters that it was a "very black day."

A black day: After word of Paul Dana's death, Rahal Letterman employees load the cars of Danica and Buddy Rice into trailers.

A New Fuel

Traditionally, IRL racers used gasoline to fuel their cars. But gasoline ignites quickly, causing some cars to shoot up in flames upon impact. And special chemicals are needed to put out a gasoline-based fire. In the 1970s, IRL racers switched to methanol, which is made from natural gas.

Methanol does not produce as much heat as gasoline and is slower to ignite. If a car catches on fire, people can put out the flames with water. In 2006 the IRL began using a blend of 90 percent methanol and 10 percent ethanol. Ethanol is a fuel made from plants such as corn, wheat, and sugarcane, and it burns cleanly. It also has safety advantages, such as being gentler than methanol on human skin.

By 2007 all IRL cars were racing on pure ethanol. The decision to use ethanol was in part to honor Paul Dana. Before his death in 2006, Paul was a leading spokesperson for ethanol.

Fill 'er up: A crew member refuels driver Jaques Lazier's car.

Wheldon wins Toyota Indy 300 to end tragic day

<u>From the Pages of</u>
<u>USA TODAY</u>

Dan Wheldon grabbed for his sunglasses—presumably to hide tears he felt welling up inside—moments before he cut short the post-race news conference for the Toyota Indy 300 at Homestead-Miami Speedway on Sunday. It was part of an emotional day that began with news that Paul Dana had been killed in practice and ended when Wheldon held off Helio Castroneves to repeat as the winner here. "On a difficult day like today, everybody came together and I think put on a great show," Wheldon said.

Wheldon, in his first race with Chip Ganassi Racing, crossed the line 0.0147 seconds, or about 3 feet [0.9 meters], ahead of Castroneves. The race was run without Danica Patrick and Buddy Rice, Dana's Rahal Letterman Racing teammates. Andretti Green Racing, which Wheldon led to its second consecutive title last season, only had one of its four cars finish on the lead lap. It was the first time in 40 races that Andretti Green didn't place a driver in the top three.

—A. J. Perez

Danica started tenth and finished eighth during the 2006 Indy 500. She was disappointed in the result, partly because she couldn't explain why she hadn't done better. She didn't make any mistakes, and the setbacks from her 2005 Indy 500 didn't repeat themselves. Her car didn't stall and she didn't spin. Danica and others on the team blamed the car's chassis for the poor finish. It was an older chassis that was not up to speed with the newer models. But even when Danica got a new chassis, she was not happy with most of her results that season. Danica had improved over her rookie year. She had seven top ten finishes and came in ninth overall. But the season still felt like a disappointment to her. She hadn't won a race. And she couldn't explain why she hadn't performed better in the Indy 500.

Back at the Brickyard: Danica *(front)* wasn't satisfied with her eighth place finish at the 2006 Indy 500.

Rumors

Rumors began to circulate that Danica was going to switch teams—and maybe even classes. Her contract with Rahal Letterman Racing was up at the end of the 2006 season. Like other race car drivers, Danica wanted to win. "It's important for me to know what's out there and who is interested in me and who will give me the best chance to win," she told the press. "NASCAR is so big, how can you ignore it?" But Danica's heart was still with the IRL. "My priorities haven't changed,"

May 26, 2006

ABC Aims to Keep Indy 500 Viewers Tracking Action

From the Pages of
USA TODAY

Danica Patrick needn't win ABC's Indianapolis 500 Sunday to give the race itself a win—in TV terms. The Indy 500, when it comes to TV ratings, seemed destined to be permanently eclipsed by NASCAR's Coca-Cola 600, which airs later the same day. Ratings for the 600, airing on Fox, first passed the 500 in 2002, and the gap widened until Patrick's debut last year. What happened then: The NASCAR race drew its best-ever rating—6.1% of U.S. TV households—but it wasn't that day's most-popular set of left turns. The 500 drew 6.5%. Sunday, ABC will carry two prerace features on Patrick before the race, when it will also devote a camera crew to follow her everywhere.

—Michael Hiestand

she claimed. "I still want to be a winning IndyCar driver. If I'm given an opportunity to drive for an IndyCar team and win races, I'm going to do it."

Although she appreciated all Bobby Rahal had done for her, it was time to move on. In July, despite all the rumors about NASCAR, Danica announced she would be joining Andretti Green Racing for the 2007 IRL season. The switch strained Danica's relationship with Bobby Rahal. "I do believe there is something called loyalty," Rahal later told the press. "I think it's fair to say had I not brought Danica in, who knows where she would be right now." Danica told *USA Today* that she "just wanted an opportunity with a team that gives [her] the best chance to win races."

#7 Motorola

Danica was ready for a fresh start. When she joined Andretti Green, Danica gained a new pit crew, new sponsors, a new car, and a new boss. Danica began her first season with Andretti Green racing the #7 Dallara Honda, sponsored by Motorola.

New wheels: Danica prepares to test-drive her #7 Motorola Dallara Honda.

July 26, 2006

Patrick to switch IRL teams in '07

From the Pages of
USA TODAY

Danica Patrick won't be switching series, but the first female driver to lead the Indianapolis 500 will be changing teams within the IRL. Patrick, 24, announced Tuesday that she signed with Andretti Green Racing [AGR] for 2007 to give herself a better shot at victory No. 1 and beyond, ending speculation she might be heading to NASCAR.

"I just wanted an opportunity with a team that gives me the best chance to win races," she told *USA Today*. Evidently that wasn't Rahal Letterman Racing, a team she has been with the last two seasons in the IRL and four overall.

AGR has won the last two IRL IndyCar Series titles, and Tony Kanaan led the team to an IRL-record 22nd team victory Sunday at the Milwaukee Mile [in Wisconsin]. Patrick will join Kanaan and Indy 500 runner-up Marco Andretti in AGR's 2007 stable. Tuesday's announcement was welcomed by the IRL's front office. "It's a good day for IndyCar Series racing, yes, but was there any doubt?" IRL spokesman John Griffin said.

NASCAR took the news in stride. "We wish Danica well with Andretti Green Racing," NASCAR spokesman Ramsey Poston said. "Our focus continues to be on those drivers committed to NASCAR, and it's shaping up to be another fantastic season."

—A. J. Perez; Contributing: Nate Ryan

In 2007, Danica started and finished the Indy 500 in eighth place. She had eleven top ten finishes that year. She set a career high at the Raceway at Belle Isle in Michigan, where she came in second place. Danica finished the season in seventh place with 424 points, her best ranking yet in the overall standings. Just as she had done during her karting days, Danica continued to improve, race after race and year after year. Although she had come close, Danica still hadn't won an IRL race. And she hadn't been able to beat her record-breaking fourth-place start and finish in the Indy 500. Danica and her fans began to wonder what it was going to take for her to win.

IN F⊙CUS

A Family Affair

Andretti Green Racing is a racing team with a strong family history. The team is co-owned by Michael Andretti (b. 1964). Michael is the son of Mario Andretti (b. 1940), one of the most famous and successful race car drivers ever. Marco Andretti (b. 1987), Michael's son, races for Andretti Green. In 2006 Marco became the IRL's Rookie of the Year.

Three generations: Mario Andretti (*left*), Marco Andretti (*middle*), and Michael Andretti (*right*) share a name associated with racing excellence.

www.usatoday.com

USA TODAY

CHAPTER SIX

The 2007 team: Danica and her new Andretti Green crew gather together at the Indianapolis Motor Speedway in 2007.

The Checkered Flag

Danica heard the question over and over again. "When are you going to win?" She couldn't answer with any certainty. How could she know? She had been doing her best. One circumstance or another had prevented her from being the first car to cross the finish line—the car that triggers the waving of the checkered flag, racing's traditional symbol of victory. But giving up was not on Danica's radar screen. She was going to win, she thought. It was just a question of when.

March 24, 2008

Danica Patrick criticizes
new IRL weight rule

From the Pages of USA TODAY

An Indy Racing League rule change has Danica Patrick feeling as if she'll be penalized for being petite — which the popular driver said wouldn't happen in other sports. Starting this season, the minimum weight for IRL cars will include the driver, and Patrick is the series' lightest at 100 pounds [45.4 kilograms].

"If someone's going to take the hit it's going to be me," Patrick said Thursday. "It's disappointing the league decided to do that. In other sports, athletes don't get penalized for being too strong, or too tall or too fast. (It's) just your God-given stature is being penalized. What am I going to do, though? It's not my decision. Maybe I'll get more specific reasons somewhere down the line."

IRL spokesman John Griffin said the rule was intended to reduce the difference between the lightest and heaviest drivers, which is a gap that can range from 75 to 100 pounds [34 kg to 45.4 kg].

"We want to make absolutely clear this is not a Danica rule," Griffin said. "You look at guys like Dan Wheldon and Marco Andretti, and they're light guys."

Griffin wouldn't disclose the cars' minimum weight but said drivers are broken into three weight classifications. The heaviest would have weight reduced from its car while the lightest would have a maximum 35 pounds [16 kg] of ballast added. An Associated Press story in 2005 reported rival teams estimated Patrick might gain nearly 1 mph [1.6 km/h] because of her weight, and Sprint Cup driver Robby Gordon said he wouldn't race Patrick in the IRL until the series equalized weights as NASCAR's premier circuit does. Patrick hopes to put the issue behind her by winning the season-opening Gainsco 300 at Homestead Miami Speedway on Saturday.

"Let's just do that," she said with a laugh, "and then I'll say, 'Why didn't you guys do this years ago?'"

—Nate Ryan

Across the Pacific

In April 2008, Danica and her family were getting ready to go to Japan to race the Indy Japan 300 at the Twin Ring Motegi oval. Motegi is a rural mountain village that lies about 65 miles (105 km) northwest of Tokyo, Japan's capital and largest city. Danica had good luck at Motegi in 2005, before her impressive performance at the Indy 500 that same year. She qualified to start in second place, on the outside of the front row. More impressively, she led the race for thirty-two of the two hundred laps. Danica had fond memories of Japan. She was looking forward to returning to the oval there. The 2008 Indy Japan 300 would be Danica's fiftieth IRL race.

IN F◉CUS

Freaky Strong

Race car drivers are strong. According to Danica, they're "freaky strong." Holding the steering wheel of an IndyCar at high speeds requires upper-body strength. It also requires endurance. Danica and other drivers must hold the wheel to fight the g-force, or the gravitational pull. The g-force in an IndyCar is twice as powerful as it is in a jet. Drivers fight the g-force the entire time they're driving, which can be up to four hours.

To stay strong, Danica works out.

She runs between forty and sixty minutes every day to help with her endurance. And she makes sure to do yoga a few times a week. Yoga poses stretch the muscles, which helps to keep them flexible. This allows her to contract (hold) them for as long as she needs to during a race without cramping up. To strengthen her upper body, Danica lifts weights. Most people who meet Danica know how strong she is. Her powerful handshake has become one of her hallmark traits.

The night before the family boarded the plane, Brooke asked her sister a question worth thinking about. "Do you really want to win in Japan? Do you really want to win an ocean away?"

Without hesitating, Danica replied "yes." Sure, it'd be more fun to win in her home country, but winning is winning. Danica was ready. It didn't matter where a win happened. What mattered to her was reaching her goal.

 Danica's family is still heavily involved in her racing career. T. J. manages several parts of Danica's racing business, including her website and merchandise. He also drives Danica's motor coach from event to event. Bev helps with business paperwork and finances. Brooke, meanwhile, is studying to become a physical therapist like her brother-in-law.

Cutting it Close

Long before the race even began at Motegi, Danica and her pit crew had a strategy. They would make sure Danica had enough fuel near the race's midway point that she wouldn't have to make a pit stop closer to the end of the race. Stops during the final laps had cost her races before. Danica was to fuel up for a final time with fifty-two laps to go, well before the end of the race. But the strategy involved some risk. The most any race car had been able to run on a tank of ethanol was fifty-one laps. Team Andretti Green was cutting it close.

The Friday before Sunday's race was qualifying day. It rained so hard, though, that qualifying rounds were canceled. Racers would have to position themselves on the track according to their championship standing. Helio Castroneves, a driver on the Penske Racing team, got pole position. Danica would be starting in sixth place.

Flag Language

For race car drivers, the black-and-white checkered flag is a symbol of victory. As soon as the first driver crosses the finish line, the marshal waves the flag before drivers and cheering fans.

The IRL uses a total of eleven different flags to communicate with drivers—more than any other race car league in the world.

Green: A green flag means "go!" It's used to start races, qualifying sessions, and practices.

White: A white flag signals that the lead driver has entered the last lap of the race.

Yellow: A yellow flag says "caution." An accident has happened or a hazardous object is on the track. When the yellow flag is waving, drivers must slow down. They are not allowed to pass one another unless they are headed to their pit to refuel and re-tire.

Red: A red flag means stop! Conditions on the track are unsafe.

Yellow and Red Stripes: Drivers should slow down. Dangerous conditions on the track's surface could cause accidents.

Red with Yellow X: The pit lane is closed. No driver can make a pit stop when this flag is waving.

White with a Red Cross: This is the medical flag, indicating to drivers that they must slow down and make way for an ambulance.

Black: When this flag is coupled with a number, the driver with that vehicle number needs to pull over.

Blue with a Yellow Stripe: This tells a slow driver he or she is going to be lapped by another driver.

Black with a White Cross: This flag tells a driver that he or she has been disqualified.

Black-and-White Checkered: The race's winner has crossed the finish line.

We have a winnner: A race's marshall waves the checkered flag once the first driver crosses the finish line.

Tears of Joy

Saturday was a good day for a race in Motegi. Clouds still hung in the air, but it was dry—a huge improvement over the wet and rainy qualifying day in the village. As always, Danica geared up and psyched up for the race. She reviewed the strategy with her team, put on her track face, and got in the car.

For most of the race, Danica kept her sixth-place spot. With fifty-seven laps remaining, the yellow caution flag appeared. Most drivers, including Danica and Helio Castroneves, stopped to fill up their fuel cells. Only five laps later, Danica and Castroneves made yet another pit stop to refuel. This would be their last scheduled pit stop.

Leading the pack: Danica had enjoyed success in Japan prior to the 2008 Indy Japan 300. In 2005, she *(front left)* led the Indy Japan 300 for thirty-two laps.

Heavy News

At just under 5 feet 2 inches (157 centimeters) tall and weighing in at about 100 pounds (45 kilograms), Danica has a small frame. Other racers have argued that this gives her an unfair advantage on the track. Engineers have calculated that for every 10 pounds (4.5 kg), a racer can gain (or lose) one-tenth of a mile (0.16 km) in speed. Danica is the lightest racer in the IRL. She weighs 65 pounds (29 kg) less than the heaviest male racer.

Danica admits that her weight gives her a slight advantage but takes into account other factors. "What I lack in weight, I have to more than make up for in body strength. Should I complain that men are stronger than I am and therefore they have an unfair advantage driving? I don't think so."

In 2008 the IRL passed a new rule to help balance the weight difference among drivers. For Danica, this meant adding 35 pounds (16 kg) of ballast (heavy material) to her car.

A small advantage: Danica is much shorter and lighter than many of her competitors.

At lap 197, the lead racers were forced to make a pit stop to re-fuel, and Danica jumped to second place. Castroneves was in first. Soon, Castroneves slowed his car to save fuel. At the risk of running dry, Danica passed him, and for the last three laps, she held the lead. Danica crossed the finish line and the checkered flag appeared. The strategy worked. Danica had won. On April 20, 2008, Danica Patrick became the first female winner in IRL history.

During the victory lap, when the winner of the race is paraded around the track, Danica was so filled with joy she couldn't help but cry. At first she was embarrassed, but Danica decided not to hide her tears. They were tears of joy, after all. And she had earned them.

Fly the checkered flag: Danica takes first place in Motegi in 2008, becoming the first woman to win an IRL race.

Danica won her first IRL race in 2008, the same year the league required her to add weight to her car so she wouldn't have an unfair advantage.

Danica, her crew, family, friends, and fans couldn't have been happier. Because of the time difference between Japan and the United States, the news of Danica's win reached only a small U.S. audience in the wee hours of the morning. Hours later, U.S. fans were well informed—Danica was all over the news. Danica was right about what she told her sister. A win is a win, regardless of where it happens.

Tears of joy: Danica and her mother share an emotional moment after the win at the 2008 Indy Japan 300.

Ads and Influence

Danica's success has set an example for many girl kart drivers who would like to become professional racers. If she can do it, they can do it too. In the twenty-first century, more girls than ever are entering the sport of karting. Because of women such as Janet Guthrie, Lyn St. James, Sarah Fisher, Danica Patrick, and Milka Duno, women on the racetrack may soon become commonplace. Lyn St. James has already noticed an increase in girl racers. "Young girls represent a significant number of racers in go-karts . . . and other grassroots forms of racing," she says. "And they're not just racing, they're winning. With role models like Danica, I believe we'll see the sport grow."

Victory at last: Danica stands with her 2008 Indy Japan 300 first-place trophy. She also won 95,000 dollars out of a 1,185,000-dollar purse for placing first.

After Danica won the Indy race in Japan, the governor of Illinois honored her with her own day. April 26, 2008, was Danica Patrick Day in Illinois.

Good company: Danica poses with other successful athletes, including drivers Milka Duno *(far left)*, Sarah Fisher *(second from left)*, and Lyn St. James *(center)*, as well as with tennis legend Billie Jean King *(second from right)*.

Danica's status as a professional athlete and role model comes with great respon-sibility. As Bobby Rahal once put it, Danica lives in a "fishbowl." People have a constant view of her life. She has little privacy, and people pay at-tention to how she behaves on and off the track. Many of the people watch-ing are young girls who want to be just like Danica.

USA TODAY Snapshots®

Who is America's favorite female sports star?

1. **Serena Williams** (tennis)
2. **Venus Williams** (tennis)
3. **Danica Patrick** (auto racing)
4. **Candace Parker** (basketball)
5. **Mia Hamm** (soccer)

Source: Harris Interactive

By Matt Young and Sam Ward, USA TODAY, 2009

Danica takes this responsibility seriously, although she's careful to be true to her nature. Before endorsing, or approving of, a product through an advertisement, Danica makes sure she believes in the product. Before interviewing for a magazine, she makes sure she's proud to be featured in the publication.

Danica has been criticized for appearing in television ads and magazine photo shoots in which she shows off her sexier side. Some people claim that Danica is capitalizing on her good looks at the expense of women. Her ads and photo shoots make it more difficult for women racers to be taken seriously, they argue. They believe that Danica is being exploited.

Danica's critics would rather she be noticed for her athletic ability. Danica says she wants the same thing. But because Danica is always hiding her feminine side on the track, her appearances in ads and magazines are a way to show the public the feminine side she rarely, if ever, shows as a driver. Danica doesn't apologize for her endorsement deals. She doesn't deny that she earns a great deal of money by appearing in advertisements, either. For Danica, the ads are part of the business.

Raise a glass: Danica stands next to a poster featuring her "Got Milk?" ad at a 2009 press conference.

April 24, 2008

Generation of girls gets new mentor

<u>From the Pages of USA TODAY</u> The news reached one father and his 12-year-old daughter while they were at a race track in Santa Maria, Calif., fine-tuning the girl's go-kart. The man's cellphone rang: "Danica just won her first race." The daughter's eyes grew wide with joy. Another father and his 12-year-old girl were walking along a sidewalk while attending the Long Beach Grand Prix when they happened to look through the picture window of a bar to see the Indy-car race in Japan on a big-screen TV.

"There were five laps to go," said Matt Fenaroli, "so we stopped and watched through the window. We just stood there on the sidewalk, jumping up and down, chanting, 'Don't run out of gas! Don't run out of gas!' It was a great moment for us."

They exist in a world unknown to the mainstream sports media, these people who cheered the loudest for Danica Patrick's historic victory last weekend. They thrive in the vast proving ground of the hugely popular sport of auto racing, where girls learn to drive by the age of 5 and go from zero to 80 by the age of 12.

"So many are out there under the radar screen," said Lyn St. James, seven-time Indy 500 racer who has helped guide more than 200 girls and young women through her Driver Development Program over the past 14 years.

"Somewhere between 15 and 20% of all young kids racing today are girls," she said. "Danica's victory is so empowering to them. She has eliminated the question in the minds of many: Can a woman win at the top level? It's tough, but what Danica did helps a lot."

If one can imagine the auto racing world in another 10 years with another three or four women racing in the IndyCar series, or perhaps even NASCAR, one of those women might be Raquel "Rocky" Martinez of East Los Angeles [California], or Natalie Fenaroli of Kansas City [Missouri].

Today, they are where Danica was when she was about their age, mentored by St. James. They win their regional and national titles by beating the boys, mostly, at tracks in Oklahoma, Missouri and California.

"There's no slack cut to her because she's a girl," said [Natalie Fenaroli's] father. "She gets to take the boys on straight up. It doesn't matter if it's a boy or girl in that car. The steering wheel doesn't know. She likes that and we like that."

"My daughter already has gotten to the point where it's not about being a girl, it's about being the better driver," said Raul Martinez. "It doesn't matter boy or girl, it's the best driver who wins. Just like what Danica did. End of story."

—Christine Brennan

Giving back: Danica talks to 10-year-old Taegan Poles, a Canadian karter, about horsepower at the Toronto Auto Show in 2009.

Racing Future

Danica ended the 2008 season in sixth place, an improvement over her 2007 seventh-place finish. And as the first woman to win an Indy race, Danica had set another record. Some people thought that the win in Motegi was good enough for Danica. It wasn't the Indy 500, but it was an important race nonetheless. Rumors about Danica moving to NASCAR and even Formula One continued into 2009. But in September 2009, near the conclusion of her fifth season in the IRL, Danica signed another three-year contract with Andretti Autosport (formerly Andretti Green).

Danica finished the 2009 season in fifth place, one place better than 2008. In December 2009, she unveiled the new GoDaddy.com-sponsored IndyCar. (This car, like her last one, bears the number seven.) Danica also told fans that she had made an additional racing commitment—this one with NASCAR. In 2010 Danica signed with JR Motorsports, a NASCAR team partially owned by Dale Earnhardt Jr.

Switching from the IRL to NASCAR is no easy shift. An open-wheel vehicle handles much differently than a stock car. Many successful IRL

Double vision: Danica stands between her stock car *(left)* and her IndyCar *(right)* after announcing her deal with JR Motorsports.

Rough going: Danica rounds a corner at Auto Club Speedway in Fontana, California, on February 20, 2010. She finished the race, the Nationwide Stater Bros. 300, in thirty-first place.

drivers, including Sam Hornish Jr., have experienced limited success in NASCAR. It's not that one class of drivers is more talented than another. It's that each racing class requires a different set of skills and lots of experience. Jimmie Johnson, winner of NASCAR's Sprint Cup championship in 2006, 2007, 2008, and 2009, has cautioned open-wheel drivers about moving to stock cars. Johnson advises racers to stay in the IRL and practice driving a stock car in the minor leagues before committing to the change.

Danica has followed Johnson's advice. In the winter of 2010, she began driving her #7 GoDaddy.com Chevrolet in minor league events. Her first stock car race, on February 6, 2010, was the Lucas Oil Slick Mist 200 in Daytona, Florida. The Slick Mist 200 is part of the Automobile Racing Club of America (ARCA) series for professional and semiprofessional drivers. Danica placed sixth. It was a fine start, but races later in the month did not go as smoothly. Danica competed in three races in NASCAR's Nationwide series, and placed in the thirties each time.

December 8, 2009

Patrick will take spin with NASCAR

<u>From the Pages of</u>
<u>USA TODAY</u>

The most popular drivers in NASCAR and IndyCar are joining forces.

IndyCar star Danica Patrick, who became the first woman to win an oval-track race in a national touring series last year, will reveal today she will drive for the NASCAR Nationwide Series team co-owned by Dale Earnhardt Jr., according to two executives involved with racing with knowledge of the deal who requested anonymity pending an official announcement.

Patrick will compete part time on the Nationwide circuit in 2010. The schedule, though, isn't expected to be unveiled during today's news conference in Phoenix, which is near the headquarters of GoDaddy.com, Patrick's IndyCar sponsor that also is expected to adorn her stock car.

GoDaddy.com CEO Bob Parsons will join Patrick at the announcement, as will Kelley Earnhardt, general manager and co-owner of JR Motorsports, who negotiated the NASCAR deal with Patrick's representatives at IMG. Earnhardt's younger brother, Dale, who was named the most popular driver in Sprint Cup for the seventh consecutive season last week, isn't expected to attend.

Patrick is planning to test a stock car Dec. 18-20 at Daytona International Speedway for the ARCA Series race (NASCAR has banned testing in its series) at the track Feb. 6.

Patrick recently signed a three-year deal to remain with Andretti Autosport in IndyCar. During a teleconference last week, she said the contract permitted NASCAR racing before and after IndyCar, which runs from March to October next year. NASCAR will begin its season at Daytona in mid-February and conclude in November. "I'd like to just try it and see how I get on with the cars," Patrick said. "I just think the racing looks fun."

—Nate Ryan

Danica continues to race part-time in the minor leagues. If she does well enough over the next few years, she may advance to NASCAR's Sprint Cup series. (The Sprint Cup series is the major league of stock car racing.) But for now, Danica says, "I'd like to just try it and see how I get on with the cars."

 What will Danica do when she decides to quit racing? She has always had a passion for clothes and accessories. And when Danica retires, she hopes to become a fashion designer and to create her own line of clothing.

Danica has already accomplished quite a few "firsts" for a female driver. As a young girl in England, she fought for and earned her rightful place in the world of racing. In North America, she earned the highest finish for a woman in the Indy 500. And in Japan, she became the first woman to win an Indy race. Danica has performed well in the sport of her dreams. But some fans believe that Danica still has at least one childhood dream to fulfill. "I still love IndyCar, and I still want to win the Indy 500," Danica told reporters after the NASCAR announcement. "I had a feeling years ago that I'm going to win this race, and I still think I will." For Danica, seeing the wave of the checkered flag at an Indy 500 would be the greatest spectacle of all.

TRACKS OF THE INDY RACING LEAGUE

Open-wheel races take place on many different kinds of racetracks, but most IRL courses are oval-shaped. In the mid-2000s, the IndyCar series also added some permanent road courses to its schedule.

Chicagoland Speedway
Joliet, Illinois
Oval, 1 1/2 mi (2.4 km)

Michigan International Speedway
Brooklyn, Michigan
Oval, 2 mi (3.2 km)

Homestead-Miami Speedway
Homestead, Florida
Oval, 1 1/2 mi (2.4 km)

Milwaukee Mile
Milwaukee, Wisconsin
Oval, 1 mi (1.6 km)

Indianapolis Motor Speedway
Speedway, Indiana
Oval, 2 1/2 mi (4 km)

Texas Motor Speeedway
Fort Worth, Texas
Oval, 1 1/2 mi (2.4 km)

Infineon Raceway
Sonoma, California
Permanent Road Course
Just less than 2 mi (3.1 km)

Watkins Glen International
Watkins Glen, NY
Permanent Road Course
Just less than 2 1/2 mi (4 km)

TIMELINE AND CAREER HIGHLIGHTS

1982   Danica Patrick is born on March 25 in Beloit, Wisconsin.

1992   After convincing their parents to purchase racing karts, Danica and her sister Brooke join the World Karting Association *(below)*. Danica finishes her first-ever racing season in second place.

1993   Danica finishes the WKA Midwest Sprint Series in second place in the Yamaha and US820 classes. She finishes fourth in the WKA Manufacturer's Cup in the Yamaha Sportsman class.

1994   Danica captures her first national championship, taking the WKA Manufacturer's Cup in the Yamaha Sportsman class. She also collects the WKA Grand National Championship in the Yamaha class and wins the WKA Great Lakes Sprint Series in the Yamaha Sportsman and US820 Sportsman classes.

1995   Danica wins the WKA Great Lakes Sprint Series title in the Yamaha Restricted Junior and US820 Junior classes. She places second in the WKA Manufacturer's Cup in the same categories.

1996 Danica is accepted into the Lyn St. James Foundation Driver Development Program. She takes the WKA Manufacturer's Cup in the Yamaha Junior class and Restricted Junior class. Danica is Manufacturer's Cup runner-up in the HPV Junior class and the WKA Grand National Championship runner-up in the Yamaha Restricted Junior class. She also captures five WKA Great Lakes Sprint Series and WKA Midwest Spring Series titles.

1997 Danica takes the WKA Grand National Championship title in the HPV class and Yamaha Lite class. She also wins the WKA Summer National Championship in the Yamaha Lite class. Danica attends the Indy 500 for the first time as a spectator.

1998 Danica begins to train in England *(below)* and races part of the Formula Vauxhall Winter Series.

1999 Danica races the full Formula Vauxhall series. She finishes ninth in the Formula Vauxhall Championship.

2000 Danica races in England's prestigious Formula Ford series. At the Formula Ford Festival, she places second, the highest-ever finish for a female driver in festival history.

2001 The Ford Motor Company ends its sponsorship of Danica. She returns to the United States and begins to look for a position on an open-wheel team.

2002 Danica wins in the pro division at the Toyota Pro/Celebrity fundraising race in Long Beach, California. Bobby Rahal gives Danica a spot on Team Rahal Racing. Danica races the Barber Dodge Pro Series, with a highest finish of fourth place in Vancouver, Canada.

2003 Danica races the Toyota Atlantic Championship Series. She becomes the first woman to race in the series full-time and ends the series in sixth place. Danica also posts five top-five finishes.

2004 Danica finishes the Atlantic Championship Series in third place. During the season, she becomes the first female driver to lead in points (reaching first in the standings) or win a pole position.

2005 Danica begins to race in the Indy Racing League's IndyCar Series. Danica becomes the first woman ever to lead a lap in the Indy 500 *(below)*. She finishes the Indy 500 in fourth place, finishes twelfth overall in the IRL, and receives several awards including Indianapolis 500 Rookie of the Year. Danica also marries Paul Hospenthal.

2006 Danica's autobiography, *Crossing the Line*, is published. Danica finishes eighth at the Indy 500 and ends the season in ninth. She announces her move from Rahal Letterman Racing to Andretti Green Racing for the 2007 IRL season.

2007   Danica begins to race in the #7 Motorola for Andretti Green. She once again finishes eighth at the Indy 500, and finishes second at the Raceway at Belle Isle, Michigan. Danica ends the season in seventh.

2008   Danica enjoys her first victory at the Indy Japan 300 in Motegi, Japan *(below)*. She ends the season in sixth place and finishes twenty-second at the Indy 500. She also receives a Nickelodeon Kids' Choice Award for Favorite Female Athlete.

2009   Danica finishes the 2009 IndyCar season in fifth place. She also finishes the Indy 500 in third, the highest finish by a woman in the event's history. Danica signs another three-year contract with Andretti Green Racing and unveils the new #7 GoDaddy.com-sponsored IndyCar. She also announces her plan to compete part-time in NASCAR.

2010   Danica begins to drive the #7 GoDaddy.com Chevrolet for JR Motorsports in both the ARCA Series and the NASCAR Nationwide Series. She also continues to compete in the IRL as a part of Andretti Green Racing.

GLOSSARY

chassis: the frame and machinery of a car

circuit: a series of races held on different tracks. Also used to mean the course, or path, a race takes.

developmental racing: series of races that inexperienced drivers can enter to get driving experience

ethanol: fuel made from a crop, such as corn or sugarcane

fuel cell: an inflatable pouch made of very durable rubber that holds fuel

g-force: the gravitational pull. A measurement of how much an object resists the earth's gravitational pull.

go-kart: a small, one-seated vehicle. Go-karts can be made for recreational purposes or for racing. Go-karts are also called karts.

karting: racing in a go-kart, or kart

lap: one time around an oval track

open-wheel racing: a race that has only open-wheel cars. Formula One and Indy Racing League sponsor the most popular open-wheel races in the world.

pit stop: a stop to refuel, change tires, or to repair a race car

Pit stop: Danica's crew changes tires during a pit stop at the 2005 Indy 500 in Indianapolis, Indiana.

pole position: the first and most favorable starting position on the track

pole-sitter: the person in the pole position

purse: the amount of money a driver can win

qualifying rounds: timed practice runs before a race. Qualifying rounds determine which drivers will race and what position they will start in

rookie: a driver who is competing in his or her first season of racing for a particular series

speedway: racetrack

straightaway: the straight portions of an oval track

strategy: a plan for how to race

throttle: accelerator, or gas pedal

SOURCE NOTES

4   Baukus Mello, Tara. *Danica Patrick* (New York: Chelsea House Publishers, 2008), 13.

12   Patrick, Danica, with Laura Morton. *Danica: Crossing the Line* (New York: Simon and Schuster, 2006), 17.

13–14   Ibid., 5.

18   Ibid., 22.

18   Weir, Tom. "Danica plans to deliver at Indy," USA Today.com, May 15, 2005, http://www.usatoday.com/sports/motor/irl/ indy500/2005-05-23-cover-patrick_x.htm (February 11, 2010).

24   "Danica Patrick seeks path to the top in 2002," Autoracing1.com, April 2002, http://www.autoracing1.com/htmfiles/2002/CART/ 0401DanicaPR.htm (September 29, 2009).

25   Patrick, 13.

31   Ibid., 72.

33   Patrick, 67.

35   Ibid., 93.

35   Weir.

41   Bobby Rahal, foreword, *Danica: Crossing the Line*, xi.

48   Patrick, 3.

51   Ibid., 39.

57   Ibid., 56.

63   Ibid., 147.

64   Ibid., 140.

65   Ibid.

65   Ibid., 125.

70   Bobby Rahal quoted in "Dana Killed in Pre-race Practice; Wheldon Wins Event," ESPN.com: IndyCar, March 27, 2006, http://sports .espn.go.com/rpm/news/story?seriesId=1&id=2385329 (February 11, 2010).

73–74   Danica Patrick quoted in "Danica's NASCAR Comments Come After Frustrating IndyCar Season," USAToday.com, June 12, 2006, http:// www.usatoday.com/sports/motor/nascar/2006-07-11-danica -nascar_x.htm (February 11, 2010).

74   Bobby Rahal quoted in "Patrick's a Power in NASCAR and IndyCar," SI Mobile, December 16, 2009, http://m.si.com/news/archive/

archive/detail/2127265/full;jsessionid
=CAAB4ABD626DDC90289CE61391798FA6.cnnsi1
(February 11, 2010).

75 Danica Patrick quoted in "Patrick moving to Andretti Green for '07
    IRL season," USAToday.com, July 25, 2006, http://www.usatoday
    .com/sports/motor/irl/2006-07-25-patrick-andretti_x.htm (April
    28, 2010).

78 John Oreovicz, "Danica Quiets Her Critics with Landmark Victory in
    Japan," ESPN.com: IndyCar, April 19, 2008, http://sports.espn
    .go.com/espn/print?id=3355243&type=Columnist&imagesPrint=off
    (September 3, 2009).

80 Patrick, 44.

81 Danica Patrick quoted in "Danica Patrick: My One on One with
    Her After the Win," Sports Biz with Darren Rovell, April 21, 2008,
    http://www.cnbc.com/id/24237863 (February 11, 2010).

84 Patrick, 175.

87 Lyn St. James, foreword. *Danica Patrick: America's Hottest Racer*
    (Saint Paul: Motorbooks, 2005), 6.

88 Bobby Rahal quoted in "Danica's come a long way on track, in life,"
    NBC Sports: Motorsports, May 27, 2006, http://nbcsports.msnbc
    .com/id/12997252/ (April 28, 2010).

95 Danica Patrick quoted in "Danica Patrick Still Flirting With
    NASCAR," Motorsports Fanhouse, December 1, 2009, http://
    motorsports.fanhouse.com/2009/12/01/danica-patrick-still-flirting
    -with-nascar/ (April 28, 2010).

95 Danica Patrick quoted in "Patrick's schedule still being set,"
    ESPN.com: NASCAR, December 18, 2009, http://sports.espn
    .go.com/rpm/nascar/news/story?id=4751040 (April 28, 2010).

95 Ibid.

SELECTED BIBLIOGRAPHY

Anderson, Lars. "Forget the Hype." Sports Illustrated Vault. May 19, 2008. Available online at *SI.com*, http://sportsillustrated.cnn.com/vault/article/magazine/MAG1137271/index.htm (September 29, 2009).

Associated Press, "Danica Patrick becomes 1st female IRL winner," Fox Sports. April 20, 2009. Available online at *Fox Sports on MSN*, http://msn.foxsports.com/other/story/8051728 (September 3, 2009).

Gifford, Clive. *Racing: The Ultimate Motorsports Encyclopedia*. Boston: Kingfisher, 2006.

IndyCar Series. http://www.indycar.com (October 14, 2009).

Ingram, Jonathan, and Paul Webb. *Danica Patrick: America's Hottest Racer*. St. Paul, MN: Motorbooks, 2008.

Panzariu, Ovidiu. "Race Flags – Indy Racing League." July 2, 2009. Available online at *autoevolution*, http://www.autoevolution.com/news/race-flags-indy-racing-league-8367.html (September 4, 2009).

Patrick, Danica, with Laura Morton. *Danica: Crossing the Line*. New York: Fireside, 2006.

Weir, Tom. "Danica plans to deliver at Indy," *USA Today*, May 23, 2005.

Young Stiers, Lisa. "Danica Patrick Races into Town for Her Third Running in the Indianapolis 500," *Indy's Child Parenting Magazine*, May 1, 2007.

FURTHER READING AND WEBSITES

Books
Baukus Mello, Tara. *Danica Patrick*. New York: Chelsea House Publishers, 2008.

Daly, Derek. *Race to Win: How to Become a Complete Champion Driver*. Saint Paul: Motorbooks, 2008.

Doeden, Matt. *Dale Earnhardt Jr*. Minneapolis: Twenty-First Century Books. 2005.

———. *Stock Cars*. Minneapolis: Lerner Publications, 2007.

Hembree, Michael. *'Then Tony Said to Junior...': The Best NASCAR Stories Ever Told*. Chicago: Triumph, 2009.

Kramer, Ralph. *Indianapolis Motor Speedway: 100 Years of Racing*. Iola, WI: Krause, 2009.

Piehl, Janet. *Formula One Race Cars*. Minneapolis: Lerner Publications Company, 2007.

———. *Indy Race Cars*. Minneapolis: Lerner Publications Company, 2007.

Rappoport, Ken. *Ladies First: Women Athletes Who Made a Difference*. Atlanta: Peachtree, 2005.

Roselius, J. Chris. *Danica Patrick: Racing to History*. Berkeley Heights, NJ: Enslow Publishers, 2009.

St. James, Lyn. *Ride of Your Life: A Race Car Driver's Journey*. New York: Hyperion, 2002.

Websites
Danica Patrick on Twitter
http://twitter.com/DanicaPatrick
This online social networking site provides updates from Danica and helps fans find out what's on her mind.

IndyCar.com
http://www.indycar.com/
The official website of the Indy Racing League, with news, race results, driver profiles, and more.

International Kart Federation (IKF)
http://www.ikfkarting.com/
The IKF, like the WKA, helps to govern the sport of karting and sponsors races throughout the United States and Canada.

Lyn St. James Academy
http://www.lynstjames.com/academy
Check out information about the developmental training Danica Patrick received—or fill out an application.

NASCAR
http://www.nascar.com
The official website of the National Association for Stock Car Auto Racing, with news, race results, a fantasy racing league, and more.

The Official Website of Danica Patrick
http://danicaracing.com/
Visit Danica's official web site to see the latest news about Danica's races, read Danica's journal entries, view race photos, and hear some inspirational music for the competitive spirit.

World Karting Association (WKA)
http://www.worldkarting.com
If you're interested in karting, check out the WKA website to learn details about events and how to get started.

INDEX

PHOTO ACKNOWLEDGMENTS

The images in this book are used with the permission of: © Darrell Ingham/ Getty Images, pp. 1, 78; © AJ Mast/USA TODAY, pp. 3, 20; © Tannen Maury/ CORBIS, p. 4; © Greg Griffo, Indianapolis Star/USA TODAY, p. 5; AP Photo/ Darron Cummings, pp. 6, 88; © Chris Graythen/Getty Images, pp. 7 (top), 16, 19, 28, 36, 43 (top), 44, 58 (top), 61 (top), 62, 72, 74, 75, 76, 79, 90, 94; AP Photo, p. 7 (bottom); © Matt Detrich, Indianapolis Star/USA TODAY, pp. 8, 10, 61 (bottom); © Bettmann/CORBIS, p. 9; © Scott Olson/Getty Images, p. 11; © Jonathan Ferrey/Getty Images, pp. 12, 42, 59, 87, 89; © Alexander Hubrich/ CORBIS, pp. 14, 97; AP Photo/Tom Strattman, p. 17; © Tim Dillon/USA TODAY, p. 18; Seth Poppel Yearbook Library, p. 21; © Sutton Motorsports/ZUMA Press, pp. 24, 25, 30, 31, 34 (both), 98; © Jason Smith/Getty Images for NASCAR/USA TODAY, p. 26; © Ford Motors/Getty Images, p. 27; © Mark Thompson/Getty Images, p. 29; © Robert Laberge/Getty Images, pp. 35, 64, 73; © Lesley Ann Miller/ZUMA Press, pp. 38, 57, 99; AP Photo/Mark J. Terrill, p. 40; © Sam Riche, Indianapolis Star/USA TODAY, p. 43 (bottom); © Jim Spellman/WireImage/ Getty Images, p. 45; Sutton-Images.com, pp. 46, 47; © Craig Peterson/Icon SMI/ ZUMA Press, p. 48; AP Photo/Luis M. Alvarez, pp. 50, 70 (both); AP Photo/Mark Baker, p. 51; © Gavin Lawrence/Getty Images, p. 52; AP Photo/Chuck Robinson, pp. 53, 101; AP Photo/Seth Rossman, p. 54; AP Photo/Michael Conroy, p. 55; REUTERS/Geoff Miller, p. 56; REUTERS/Larry Papke, p. 58 (bottom); © Matt Kryger, Indianapolis Star/USA TODAY, p. 65; © Billy Kingsley, The Tennessean/USA TODAY, p. 66; AP Photo/Jennifer Graylock, p. 68; AP Photo/ Doug McSchooler, p. 71; AP Photo/Paul Kizzle, p. 77; © Mike Powell/Getty Images, p. 82; © Michael Kim/CORBIS, p. 83; AP Photo/Shuji Kajiyama, pp. 84, 86; AP Photo/Katsumi Kasahara, pp. 85, 100; © Keith Beaty/The Toronto Star/ ZUMA Press, p. 91; © Joshua Lott/Getty Images, p. 92; AP Photo/Alex Gallardo, p. 93; © Laura Westlund/Independent Picture Service, p. 96.

Front cover: © Rusty Jarrett/Getty Images.
Back cover: © Andrew P. Scott/USA TODAY.

ABOUT THE AUTHOR

Karen Sirvaitis is an author and editor who has written more than twenty books, including *Barack Obama: A Leader in a Time of Change*, another contribution to the USA TODAY Lifeline Biographies series. She lives in northwestern Wisconsin.